Question Based
Bible Study Guide

Answers
to Tough
Questions

Good Questions
Have Groups Talking

By Josh Hunt

Contents

Answers, Lesson #1
Defending the Faith
Jude 1 – 4; 20 - 25
Good Questions Have Groups Talking
www.joshhunt.com

Email your folks and ask them to read the entire book of Jude (all one chapter). In addition, if they have a Study Bible, read the introduction and any notes they might have. What a delight it is to discuss with an informed, prepared group.

OPEN

What is one thing you are grateful for today?

DIG

1. What do you know about Jude, the man?

The author gives his name and identifies himself as James's brother: "Jude, a bondservant of Jesus Christ, and brother of James, to those who are called, sanctified by God the Father, and preserved in Jesus Christ" (Jude 1).

There are two major views as to which Jude wrote this book. Some feel Jude is the physical half brother of Jesus, because the author identifies himself as the brother of James (another physical half brother of Jesus). He refers to apostles as "they" (Jude 1:17–18), and has strong Jewish content. However, other people feel this is the Jude who was the apostle, that is, "Judas . . . not Iscariot" (John 14:22). This Judas remained faithful when Judas Iscariot denied the Lord and sinned. Because of Judas's faithfulness and his name, this Judas was very aware of false teaching and treachery. As he traveled throughout the early church, people rejected this Judas because of his name, which reminded them of Judas Iscariot. So he changed his name to Lebbaeus Thaddaeus (Matt. 10:3). A change of name removed barriers from his preaching the gospel. Therefore, this Judas would have understood the barriers of false teaching against which he wrote. However, later in life, Lebbaeus Thaddaeus changed his name back to Judas, or Jude. (Remember Judah is the Hebrew name, Judas is the Greek name, and Jude is the Latin name, the same name with different pronunciations and spellings.) He changed his name back because he was ministering to Latins. The early church called this man Trionomous, "the man with three names." — Elmer L. Towns, *Bible Answers for Almost All Your Questions* (Nashville: Thomas Nelson, 2003).

2. What do we know about the book of Jude?

There is no obscurity in Jude's purpose. He wished to discuss facets of salvation, but the threat of subversive teachers compelled him to write and exhort his readers "to contend earnestly for the faith" (v. 3). Thus the entire epistle is an assessment of false teachers and a strong warning to the recipients. The false teachers reject Christ's authority, but Jude stresses that Jesus is Lord, now and forever. Therefore, He is to be followed both in doctrine and deed. — W. A. Criswell et al., eds.,

Believer's Study Bible, electronic ed. (Nashville: Thomas Nelson, 1991), Jud 1.

3. What would you say is the key verse in this short book?

What is the message of Jude?

Jude was warning of dangerous libertines who were living ungodly lives, and their lives were destroying their doctrine. But he also warned of false doctrine and laid the foundation with negative examples of moral obedience, like Sodom and Gomorrah and the disobedient angels who sinned in the beginning.

What are the key words in Jude?

The key words are contend for the faith. Throughout this book the author wants people to fight against heresy, go to war against sin, and engage false teachers who are attacking their faith.

What is the key verse in Jude?

"Beloved, while I was very diligent to write to you concerning our common salvation, I found it necessary to write to you exhorting you to contend earnestly for the faith which was once for all delivered to the saints" (Jude 1:3). — Elmer L. Towns, *Bible Answers for Almost All Your Questions* (Nashville: Thomas Nelson, 2003).

4. What does it mean to contend for the faith?

The word translated "contend," when verbalized, sounds like our word agonizing. It possesses the idea of athletes who, in an effort to win, find themselves intensely struggling, competing, even fighting with all their might. Interestingly, the word also seems to attach itself to things that are intrinsically worthy of full-orbed and all-engaging effort. Or, as a Greek-English Lexicon puts it, "effort expended ... in a noble cause."3

"Effort expended ... in a noble cause." This is what Jude is after. He aims at enlivening the church of his day to an immediate and intense struggle, a very real fight requiring all of their available energy. So, what does this early observation mean for us? — David R. Helm, *1 & 2 Peter and Jude: Sharing Christ's Sufferings, Preaching the Word* (Wheaton, IL: Crossway Books, 2008), 295.

5. **A closely related word is used in 1 Corinthians 9.25. (This exactly word is used only here in the New Testament.) What do we learn about Christian living from 1 Corinthians 9.25?**

I am convinced that if the apostle Paul were on earth today, he would be an avid sports fan. Paul saw powerful parallels between the discipline needed for athletic competition and the endurance required to live the Christian life. Both endeavors call for an intense, single-minded focus on winning. Both demand hard work and rigorous training. At the end of the Christian race here on earth just like at the end of an athletic event, those who have run with endurance receive a reward. — Douglas Connelly, *Heaven: Finding Our True Home: 8 Studies for Individuals or Groups: With Notes for Leaders, A LifeGuide Bible Study* (Downers Grove, IL: IVP Connect: An Imprint of InterVarsity Press, 2000), 21.

6. **What can sports teach us about discipleship?**

PAUL takes another line. He insists to those Corinthians who wanted to take the easy way that no one will ever get anywhere without the sternest self-discipline. Paul was always fascinated by the picture of the athlete. An athlete must train with intensity in order to win the contest; and Corinth knew how thrilling contests could be, for at Corinth the Isthmian Games, second only to the Olympic Games, were held. Furthermore, the athlete undergoes this self-discipline and this training to win a crown of laurel leaves that within days will be a withered wreath. How much more should Christians discipline themselves to win the crown which is eternal life? — William Barclay, *The Letters to the Corinthians, 3rd ed., The New Daily Study Bible* (Louisville, KY; London: Westminster John Knox Press, 2002), 100.

7. What does it mean for us—you and me—to contend for the faith?

Well, for starters, understanding this to be Jude's theme changes everything for us as readers. In the last chapter we envisioned settling down with Jude in some quiet corner for uninterrupted reading. We soaked in his opening words, and they buoyed our spirits—how good it was to be reminded so unhurriedly by him of God's decided love for us.

But now, with Jude's urgent appeal in verse 3 to "contend," our mind is forced to go on red alert. We are being asked to read standing in readiness. Jude is finished with pleasantries; some required action is at hand. Urgency and immediacy move him. He wants contenders, and he wants them now. And with this letter he means to raise them up. If Jude were to write a letter to the church in our day, he wouldn't change a thing. We need this generation of Christians to contend. David R. Helm, *1 & 2 Peter and Jude: Sharing Christ's Sufferings, Preaching the Word* (Wheaton, IL: Crossway Books, 2008), 295–296.

8. What was Jude going to write about—before he changed his mind?

Jude did not set out to compose this particular letter. He had wanted to write (graphein: present infinitive, which could suggest "in a leisurely manner") on the general subject of the salvation we share. That "common salvation" (KJV, RSV) was one that belonged to all believers equally. It included sharing the same Christ (Acts 4:12), the same grace (Eph. 2:8), the same justification with God (Rom. 3:22), and the same entrance by faith (2 Pet. 1:1). — Norman Hillyer, *1 and 2 Peter, Jude, Understanding the Bible Commentary Series* (Grand Rapids, MI: Baker Books, 2011), 237.

9. Verse 4. What caused Jude to change his mind?

But Jude's intention to enlarge on such themes to edify his readers was overtaken by events. News suddenly reached him that his Christian friends were threatened by a dangerous heresy. The report made him snatch up his pen there and then to write (grapsai, aorist infinitive) a very different letter from the one he had originally proposed. — Norman Hillyer, *1 and 2 Peter, Jude, Understanding the Bible Commentary Series* (Grand Rapids, MI: Baker Books, 2011), 237.

10. In the old NIV, Paul says, "I had to write." When the 2011 version came out, the translators strengthened it to, "I felt compelled to write and urge you..." What is Paul feeling here?

I had to write (anankēn eschon grapsai): The compulsion (anankēn) to write at once was as clear as if he had been given a verbal order to do so. In obedience to that inner constraint, and out of love for his Christian friends, he writes without delay to urge them to contend for the faith. The Greek word for urge is parakalōn, from parakalein, to call (kalein) alongside (para). Jude would prefer to be alongside his friends in their peril, but since he is unable to be with them in person, he does the next best thing by sending a letter. — Norman Hillyer, *1 and 2 Peter, Jude, Understanding the Bible Commentary Series* (Grand Rapids, MI: Baker Books, 2011), 237.

11. Jude 20. What exactly does it mean to build yourself up in the faith?

The infiltrators are doing their utmost to disrupt the Christian fellowship and to break it down. Jude's friends, by contrast, are to concentrate on a spiritual construction program. Build yourselves up in your most holy faith, he tells them. This is to be achieved by an ever deepening grasp of what God in Christ has done for them, according to the teaching handed down by the apostles (v. 3). Although Jude does not spell it out, this building up is the consequence of Bible study, meditating upon the word of God as recorded in the Scriptures, as other early Christian writers consistently make clear.

But it has to be borne in mind that Jude's exhortation is addressed to the whole body of believers. He is not suggesting that individuals should concern themselves only with their own spiritual progress. All have a part to play in strengthening the Christian community as a whole. The biblical metaphor of "building up, edifying" is invariably communal, not individual (1 Cor. 14:12, 26; 1 Thess. 5:11; 1 Pet. 2:5). — Norman Hillyer, *1 and 2 Peter, Jude, Understanding the Bible Commentary Series* (Grand Rapids, MI: Baker Books, 2011), 263.

12. What do we learn about Christian living from this?

The Christian life must never stand still; if it does, it will go backward. A house left to itself falls apart. The apostates are in the business of tearing down, but each Christian must be involved in building up—first, his own spiritual life and then his local assembly. — Warren W. Wiersbe, *The Bible Exposition Commentary, vol. 2* (Wheaton, IL: Victor Books, 1996), 559.

13. Let's get practical. How do you build yourself up in the faith?

How are we built up in faith? The Bible tells us very simply that faith comes by hearing and hearing by the Word of God (Romans 10:17). That's it. To keep yourself in the love of God means that you continue to be a student of the Word. You build up your faith by taking in God's Word, by daily making the practice of spending time in Scripture a priority, by assembling with other believers to study the Word corporately (Hebrews 10:25). — Jon Courson, *Jon Courson's Application Commentary* (Nashville, TN: Thomas Nelson, 2003), 1651.

14. This introduces us to our study for the next six weeks: Answers to Tough Questions. In theology, they call this the study of Apologetics. What is meant by the term Apologetics?

I teach a Sunday school class called "Defenders" to about one hundred people, from high schoolers to senior adults, at our home church in Atlanta. We talk about what the Bible teaches (Christian doctrine) and about how to defend it (Christian apologetics). Sometimes people who aren't in our class don't understand what we do. One fine Southern lady, upon hearing that I teach Christian apologetics, remarked indignantly, "I'll never apologize for my faith!"

The reason for her misunderstanding is obvious: "Apologetics" sounds like "apologize." But apologetics is not the art of telling somebody you're sorry that you're a Christian! Rather apologetics comes from the Greek word apologia, which means a defense, as in a court of law. Christian apologetics involves making a case for the truth of the Christian faith.

Apologetics comes from the Greek word apologia, which means a defense, as in a court of law. Christian apologetics involves making a case for the truth of the Christian faith.

The Bible actually commands us to have such a case ready to give to any unbeliever who wants to know why we believe what we do. Just as the contestants in a fencing match have learned both to parry each attack as well as to go on the offensive themselves, so we must always be "on guard." First Peter 3:15 says, "Always be prepared to make a defense [apologia] to anyone who asks you for a reason for the hope that is in you; yet do it with gentleness and respect" (author's translation).
— William Lane Craig, *On Guard: Defending Your Faith with Reason and Precision* (Colorado Springs, CO: David C Cook, 2010).

15. Some say, "Christian faith is a matter of life and experience not lifeless facts or reasons." You say?

Theological liberals rejected apologetics, viewing Christianity as a matter of experience and ethics, not based on objective, historical events. Acceptance of a postmodernist view of knowing rejects a rational approach to truth opting for experience as a validation of spirituality. When Christianity is interpreted as an experience unrelated to its historical origin it loses its uniqueness and can be made to mean most anything.

Experience does not establish truth. We may have a sensation of falling down some steps. It may be a dream or it may in fact be happening. Personal experience must be interpreted by truth. A true understanding of our experience is the one that corresponds to reality. We need rational evidence to establish truth so we can know that our Christian experience is not fictional mysticism but rather solid reality.

When Lee Strobel was researching for his book, The Case for Christ, a respected theologian told him, "People don't care about historical evidence for Jesus anymore. They're more persuaded by experience and community than facts and reason." Yet his book has been a phenomenal best seller. Strobel reports that the largest group of persons influenced to become Christians by his book are sixteen to twenty-four-year-olds.7 People still want to know if the gospel is true. — H. Lynn Gardner, *Commending and Defending Christian Faith: An Introduction to Christian Apologetics* (College Press Publishing Co., 2010), 230.

16. Is our faith a reasonable, logical faith?

Christian truth is verified by subjective response not by reason or history. Those who reject the correspondence view of truth holding rather to a subjective view of truth generally reject rational apologetics. Existentialist, Neo-Orthodox, and postmodern thinkers reject apologetics because they base truth on subjective experience. The increase of subjectivism, relativism, and pluralism in the last two centuries has led to the devaluation of reason and to the denial of objective truth. This type of thinking has contributed to the rejection of apologetics by non-Christians and some Christians as well.

Those who reject reason often quote Pascal's statement, "The heart has reasons, which reason does not know." Trueblood declares them mistaken because:

Pascal, being himself an unusually keen rationalist, is not their ally. When he contrasts the reasons of the heart with the reasons of the head he is not denying reason, but instead seeking to show the necessity of the involvement of the entire person. In saying that reason, as ordinarily understood, is not all there is, he is not denying but rather supplementing it, 'We know truth,' he said, 'not only by the reason, but also by the heart.' Pascal would have been the last man to make a defense of unreason.8

Arnold Lunn reasons, "No irrationalist is consistent for, if he were, he would be forced to deduce from his own premises the conclusion that all that is of interest about his conviction that objective value is unobtainable is the irrational influences which led him to this conclusion."9 Genuine Christian faith includes a subjective response, but faith does not exclude logical reasoning or evidence. — H. Lynn Gardner, *Commending and Defending Christian Faith: An Introduction to Christian Apologetics* (College Press Publishing Co., 2010), 230–231.

17. Is our faith a provable faith?

The seventh and final reason I believe in Jesus' resurrection is that the evidence for it is convincing and reasonable. There is intellectual, historical, verifiable evidence. I will not throw my brains in the trash to believe, and you do not have to either.

In a courtroom, for a case to win, it must be legally convincing beyond reasonable doubt. Today when people are tried, eyewitnesses are called to testify, experts give testimony, circumstances are examined, evidence is collected, history is reviewed, and motives are taken into account. No one on the jury was a firsthand witness to verify every specific detail of the case; however, a decision must be made. In order for a final decision to be made, the evidence must prove to be beyond a reasonable doubt. — Chip Ingram, *Why I Believe: Straight Answers to Honest Questions about God, the Bible, and Christianity* (Grand Rapids, MI: Baker, 2017).

18. Do you have any doubts about your faith that we want to explore during this study?

I will tell you my secret: I have doubts.

I have spent my life studying and thinking and reading and teaching about God. I grew up in the church. I went to a faith-based college and then to a seminary. I walked the straight and narrow. I never sowed any wild oats.

And I have doubts.

I'll tell you more than that. There is a part of me that, after I die, if it all turns out to be true — the angels are singing, death is defeated, the roll is called up yonder and there I am — there is a part of me that will be surprised. What do you know? It's all true after all. I had my doubts.

Is it okay if we ask questions and consider objections and wonder out loud?

Is it okay if we don't pretend that everybody is split up into two camps: those who doubt and those who don't?

Is it possible — maybe even rational — to have faith in the presence of doubt?

Because I have faith too. And I have bet the farm.

And faith — like doubt — grows in unexpected places. A few months ago I received an email requesting a thousand copies of a book I had written. That was an unprecedented request from anyone besides my mother, so I was curious about the story.

It was from a young man named Kirk, a high-functioning corporate type, father of three young daughters with a brilliant future before him, who found out one year ago that he had ALS — Lou Gehrig's disease.

But Kirk was convinced that in the midst of tragedy faith was his only hope. And he decided to use his final months to invite the people he loved deepest to reflect on what mattered most.

The doctors told him he had two to five years to live, but he died in nine months. I write these words on a plane returning home from a dinner that his family sponsored, with hundreds of people, where we saw a videotape of Kirk, in a wheelchair, fighting for breath, speaking of his faith in God as the only force that could sustain him.

Kirk's dad drove me to the airport. He told me of difficulties in his life — how his mother had died when he was four, how now in his seventies he had lost his son. He told me of how he had once been an agnostic, and how he had come to believe.

I do not know why tragedy, which destroys faith in some people, gives birth to it in others. Suffering both raises unanswerable questions and tells us that our only hope must be a hope beyond ourselves.

There is a mystery to faith, as there is to life, that I don't fully understand.

When we take seriously the reality of faith and doubt, the most important word in the phrase is the one in the middle.

Because most people I know are a mix of the two.

And it strikes me as arrogant when people on either side of the God-question write as if any reasonable person would agree with them because, of course, they wouldn't hold an opinion if it wasn't reasonable. — John Ortberg, *Know Doubt: Embracing Uncertainty in Your Faith* (Grand Rapids, MI: Zondervan, 2014).

19. What causes you to doubt?

If you were to ask me why I doubt, I suppose I would tell you a story about a baby as well. A couple whom I have known for a long time had a beautiful little daughter. She was the kind of child who was so beautiful that people would stop them on the street to comment on her beauty. They were the kind of parents you would hope every child might have.

They had a pool in their backyard.

One summer day it was so nice outside that the mom set up the playpen in the backyard so that her daughter could enjoy the day. The phone rang, and her daughter was in the playpen, so she went in to answer the phone. Her daughter tugged on the wall of that playpen, and the hinge that held the side up gave way. It didn't have to. God could have stopped it. God could have reached down from heaven and straightened it out and kept that playpen up. He didn't. The hinge gave way, and the side came down, and the baby crawled out, and heaven was silent.

When that mom came outside, she saw the beautiful little body of her beloved daughter at the bottom of that pool. It was the beginning of a pain that no words could name. She would have died if doing so could have changed that one moment. But she could not. She would have to live. The memory of how old her daughter would be would have to haunt her every birthday and every Christmas and on the day she would have graduated from high school. That mom would live with the emptiness, the guilt, the blame, and the aloneness.

When that little baby left this world, she left behind a world that was God-silent. — John Ortberg, *Know Doubt: Embracing Uncertainty in Your Faith* (Grand Rapids, MI: Zondervan, 2014).

20. What causes you to believe?

If you were to ask me why I believe in God, I suppose I would tell you a story about a baby. She was not the beginning of my faith in God, but she was a new chapter of it. I did not know that when a baby came into my world she would bring God with her.

When we found out baby number one was on the way, Nancy and I went through a Lamaze class together. To spare the moms-to-be anxiety, the instructors did not use the word pain. They spoke of discomfort, as in "When the baby is born, you may experience some discomfort."

On our second anniversary, Nancy began what would be twelve hours of labor. (All of our kids arrived on notable occasions, none more so than Johnny. He popped into the world on February 2, prompting the doctor to tell us that if he saw his shadow, he would go back inside and Nancy would have six more weeks of pregnancy.)

Laura's body was unusually positioned inside Nancy (the phrase the nurses used was "sunny-side up") so that the hardest part of her head was pressing against Nancy's spine. Each contraction was excruciating. The worst moment came after eleven hours and several doses of Pitocin to heighten the contractions. The doctor, with a single hand, wrenched the baby 180 degrees around inside my wife's body. Nancy let out a scream I will never forget. I knew I had to say something. "Honey — are you experiencing some discomfort?"

They finally had to use a vacuum cleaner with a special attachment to get the baby out. (The Lamaze people had warned us this procedure might make the cranium look pointed, but it would only be temporary.)

Suddenly the pain was over, and we held this little conehead in our arms and were totally unprepared for the world we had entered. Nancy, who had never been particularly attracted to anybody else's children, held the baby and looked around the room like a mother tigress. "I would kill for this baby."

I pointed out that I thought most mothers would say that they would die for their children.

"Die? Why would I want to die? If I died for her, then I couldn't be with her. I'd kill for her." And she looked around the room, clearly hoping someone would give her the chance to show she wasn't bluffing.

I took the baby from her and was overwhelmed by the wonder and mystery of the presence of a human person. Not just the mechanics of her body — though they were amazing. Not just my sudden love for this being — though it was a flood tide. What overwhelmed me was being in the presence of a new soul.

"I can't believe that there is a live, flesh-and-blood, immortal being in this room who didn't used to exist. She will grow up — and we'll watch her. She'll become a woman. And then one day she'll grow old. This red hair will turn to gray and then to white; this same skin that is so pink and smooth right now will be mottled and wrinkled, and she'll be an old lady sitting in a rocking chair — and it will be this same person," I said to Nancy.

"Yes," she said. "And I'd kill for the old lady too."

We propped that tiny body with towels and blankets in the car seat of my old VW Super Beetle to take her home. I drove like I was transporting nitroglycerin. I crawled along the freeway in the slow lane, hazard lights flashing, doing twenty-five miles per hour, ticking off motorists from Northridge to Pasadena. How do you travel carefully enough to protect a new soul?

When I held Laura, I found myself incapable of believing that she was an accident. I found myself incapable of believing that the universe was a random chaotic machine that did not care whether I loved her or hated her. I don't mean that I had a group of arguments for her having a soul and I believed those arguments. I don't mean this conviction is always present in my mind with equal force. It's not.

I mean the conviction welled up inside me and I could not get away from it. I could not look at Laura and believe otherwise. I could not hold her without saying thank you to Someone for her. I could not think of her future without praying for Someone more powerful and wiser than me to watch over her. When she arrived, she brought along with her a world that was meant to be a home for persons. A God-breathed world.

Every child is a testimony to God's desire that the world go on. — John Ortberg, *Know Doubt: Embracing Uncertainty in Your Faith* (Grand Rapids, MI: Zondervan, 2014).

21. **I'd like to invite you to join me in doing some study during the next month or so. Go on Amazon and**

do a search for Christian Apologetics. Find a book that looks interesting and read it. Your reading will strengthen your faith, and it will help the rest of us as well as you share. Anything by Lee Strobel, C.S. Lewis, Josh McDowell, Norman Geisler, or J. Warner Wallace would be great. Who is in?

22. How can we pray for each other this week?

Answers, Lesson #2
Is There a God? / Psalm 119; 111
Good Questions Have Groups Talking
www.joshhunt.com

OPEN

What is your favorite national park?

DIG

1. **Psalm 119.1 – 6. What do we learn about God from this passage?**

   Psalm 19 tells us that God speaks to us through nature which includes the numerous scientific wonders of the world. — Mark Water, *The Bible and Science Made Easy, The Made Easy Series* (Alresford, Hampshire: John Hunt Publishers Ltd, 2001), 8.

2. **Context. Psalms. How many different kinds of Psalms are there? What kind of Psalm would you say this is?**

   Students of Psalms have identified around a dozen different types of psalms. For example, there are prayers of individuals (Psalms 3:7–8), hymns celebrating God's reign over all (Psalms 47; 93–99), and royal psalms that exalt God's anointed king (Psalms 2; 20; 72). Psalm 8 is a hymn in praise of God's character and His majesty as evidenced in the glory of His creation of man. Other psalms that praise God's creation are 33, 104, and 145. It is important to note that the creation is never worshiped. Rather, God is worship for His creation. The worship of the creation rather than the Creator is a sign of the depravity of man (Romans 1:25). — David Jeremiah, *God, I Need Some Answers: Life Lessons from the Psalms (Study Guide)* (San Diego: Thomas Nelson Publishers, 2005), 18.

3. What kind of mood is David in as he writes?

In the opinion of C. S. Lewis, this is the greatest poem in the Psalter.108 There is a deep undercurrent of joy here, which disappears only briefly in verses 12 and 13. If Psalm 15 shows the conditions of fellowship with God and 16 to 18 reveal godliness in action, this reveals its basis in deep commitment to the Word of God and dependence on his power. — Geoffrey W. Grogan, *Psalms, The Two Horizons Old Testament Commentary* (Grand Rapids, MI; Cambridge, U.K.: William B. Eerdmans Publishing Company, 2008), 67–68.

4. The heaven declare the glory of God. What else declares the glory of God?

All the wonders of the heavens declare the glory of God and proclaim his exquisite handiwork. And guess what? You do too.

When you believe in God, you become a living psalm, a walking demonstration that he exists, he is faithful, and he does all things well. People will experience his presence through the words you speak, your attitude, and even your actions toward them. They will realize that the God of grace loves them and wants to illuminate their life with his joy, mercy, and salvation.

Is that what you are saying with your life? Are you shining brightly as a light to those who need God's hope? You have a story to tell, so do it well. It may make an eternal difference to those who hear you. — Baker Publishing Group, *365 Moments of Peace for a Woman's Heart: Reflections on God's Gifts of Love, Hope, and Comfort* (Grand Rapids, MI: Bethany House, 2014).

5. **Context. Look at the Psalm as a whole. It describes two ways God reveals Himself. Can you find the two ways?**

No doubt this psalm of David was inspired when, as a shepherd in Bethlehem, he looked up at the skies overhead and heard the silent sermon of the stars. Psalm 19 tells us that the reality of God can be understood in two ways: through God's creation and through His commandments. — Jon Courson, *Jon Courson's Application Commentary: Volume Two: Psalms-Malachi* (Nashville, TN: Thomas Nelson, 2006), 22.

6. **Does God speak through astrology?**

If God created the stars," she wrote me, "isn't it reasonable to believe that He wants to send us messages through them? Why shouldn't Christians practice astrology, since millions of people do?"

One reason Christians shouldn't practice astrology is, quite simply, because the Bible tells us not to. Astrology and other forms of fortune-telling were very common in the ancient world, but the Bible writers called them "detestable practices" (Deuteronomy 18:12 NIV).

Why is this? First, they knew that God did not create the stars to give us insights into the future, but to witness to

His power and glory. "The heavens declare the glory of God," the psalmist wrote.

Second, Christians don't follow astrology because we don't need to. God tells us everything we need to know about the future in His Word. Of course, the Bible doesn't tell us what will happen next week or next year; if it did, we would never learn to trust God or seek His guidance. But the Bible does tell us that the future is in God's hands and someday Christ will come again. And that is really all we need to know. — Billy Graham, *Hope for Each Day Morning and Evening Devotions* (Nashville: Thomas Nelson, 2012).

7. Why did God create the stars? What is their purpose?

God has "created all things, and by [His] will they exist and were created" (Rev. 4:11). The psalmist wrote, "The heavens declare the glory of God" (Ps. 19:1). Paul told the Ephesians that their conversions were performed "to the praise of the glory of His grace" (Eph. 1:6). The purpose of God's work is to bring glory to Himself. The responsibility of all creation is to glorify God. If in our lives and conversation we bring dishonor to God, we have failed to do the will of God. When we do what God desires, we will naturally glorify God and direct honor to Him. — Elmer L. Towns, *Bible Answers for Almost All Your Questions* (Nashville: Thomas Nelson, 2003).

8. The heavens declare the glory of God. But, so do forests and deserts and seashores. What place in nature has filled you with awe?

Moreover, it is only when we study God's great works (note the title of this series of commentaries!) that we are most moved to praise. J. B. Priestley, the author, once gazed at the Grand Canyon. Then he wrote: "I felt God had set it there as a sign. I felt wonder and awe, but at the heart of them a deep rich happiness. I had seen his handiwork and rejoiced." We praise God, moreover, because his righteousness endures for ever. Righteousness here in its feminine form means the power to love and recreate the lives of other people which God gives to those whom he has redeemed. — George Angus Fulton Knight, *Psalms, vol. 2, The Daily Study Bible Series* (Louisville, KY: Westminster John Knox Press, 2001), 185.

9. How could… (slight pause) …food cause us to worship?

God created everything, and what he created was good, but what he created to be good was not created as an end in itself but was given to us as good in order that we might be driven to worship him. In other words, when you and I take a bite of food, that should spark worship in us—not a worship of food, of course, but of the Creator of food. When you and I feel the warmth of our child hugging us, that should create worship in us. When we feel the warmth of the sun on our faces, that should create worship. When we smell the rain, that should create worship. We could go on and on. The goodness of creation is designed not to declare itself but to act as a signpost pointing heavenward. This is why Paul can say, "So, whether you eat or drink, or whatever you do, do all to the glory of God" (1 Cor. 10:31). He is working from the assumption that anything we do can be done to the glory of God. — Matt Chandler and Jared C. Wilson, *The Explicit Gospel* (Wheaton, IL: Crossway, 2012), 102–103.

10. What do the heavens—and forests and seashores—reveal about God?

AFTER SURVEYING GOD'S WORK IN CREATION, THE PSALMIST WROTE: "O LORD, how manifold are Your works! In wisdom You have made them all. The earth is full of Your possessions" (v. 24). This verse shows us important traits of God.

First, creation reveals God's wisdom. We ought to take time to admire His wisdom in creation. I've read that if the proportion of gases in the air were changed ever so slightly, all of us would die. The way God tilted the earth, the way He arranged the seasons, the way He put creation together is a revelation of His great wisdom. It's logical that the God who is wise enough to run creation is wise enough to run our lives. If He can keep the stars and the planets and the seasons and all these things going as they should, can He not put our lives together and make them what they ought to be?

Second, creation contains God's wealth. "The earth is full of Your possessions" (v. 24). Without His wealth, we could not exist. Not only are gold and silver and other precious stones measures of His wealth, but so are ore and rock, fruit and grain.

Third, creation makes possible man's work. "Man goes out to his work and to his labor until the evening" (v. 23). Even Adam had work to do in the Garden of Eden. Work is a blessing, not a burden, if we're doing it for the Lord.

Fourth, creation motivates us to worship the Lord. "O LORD, how manifold are Your works!" We don't worship creation—that's idolatry. We worship the God of creation. We recognize that He gives every good and perfect gift (James 1:17). O let us adore Him, our great Creator, our great Savior. — Warren W. Wiersbe, *Prayer, Praise & Promises: A Daily Walk through the Psalms* (Grand Rapids, MI: Baker Books, 2011), 267.

11. Read for application. What is the application of this passage?

Go outside on some clear night and just stare up into the sky for several minutes. Soak in the grandeur and majesty and vastness of the starry host—and then think: my God made all this. — Charles F. Stanley, *The Charles F. Stanley Life Principles Bible: New King James Version* (Nashville, TN: Nelson Bibles, 2005), Ps 19:1.

12. Psalm 111. Context. What do we learn about God from the Psalm as a whole?

By more than one definition, Psalm 111 is a primer of praise. As a primer can provide a brief introduction to a subject, so this psalm introduces God's praiseworthy deeds. It is the first of a trilogy of psalms beginning with the declaration, Praise the LORD (Hallelu Yah).

A primer is also a device used to teach children to read. Some have suggested that the acrostic style in which this psalm was written1 was used to help Hebrew children learn their letters. As a primer is also a thing which ignites something else, so Psalm 111 is intended to provoke an explosion of praise in the worshiper.

After the opening verse with its promise of exuberant, public and widespread praise (I will extol the LORD), the remainder of the psalm provides reasons for praise (see 111:2–10) which focus on the great works of God. That they are pondered by all who delight in them (111:2b) implies that these works are both delightful and worthy of careful study. Glorious and majestic (111:3a) translates a Hebrew play on words (also found in Psalms 45:3 and 104:1) while righteousness (111:3) refers particularly to God's actions as Vindicator of the righteous. The phrase, he has caused his wonders to be remembered (111:4a) probably alludes to God's command that Israel regularly commemorate its deliverance from Egypt,2 God's greatest demonstration of grace and compassion (see Exodus 34:6). By not specifically mentioning the Exodus, the worshiper is encouraged to consider the full scope of God's wondrous works, as typified in the Exodus.

God not only provided manna and meat for the Israelites in the wilderness, He continues to provide food for those who fear Him (Ps. 111:5).3 He showed His military might by defeating Israel's enemies and granting them the land of Canaan (111:6). He revealed His will through the Law (111:7–8), described as faithful, just, trustworthy and eternal. The creation of Israel as a nation demonstrates that God is holy and to be revered (111:9). — Stephen J. Lennox, *Psalms: A Bible Commentary in the Wesleyan Tradition* (Indianapolis, IN: Wesleyan Publishing House, 1999), 341–342.

13. Verses 9 speaks of redemption. What exactly is redemption?

Redemption (verse 9) is better translated as "ransom", as in the words of the favourite hymn, "Ransomed, healed, restored, forgiven, Who like me his praise should sing?". Note, moreover, that God sent this redemption, the verb used in the NT of God's action in Christ. Yet, even in this very verse, we are reminded of the theme of Ps. 110: Holy and terrible is his name. God's act in ransoming us comes about through the terrible judgment that his Messianic king must execute (Ps. 110:6). For a ransom has of course to be paid for. So God's greatest "work" is the forgiveness and the renewal of his people which he has "worked" at great cost to himself! — George Angus Fulton Knight, *Psalms, vol. 2, The Daily Study Bible Series* (Louisville, KY: Westminster John Knox Press, 2001), 186.

14. Verse 9. Holy is His name. What comes to mind when you hear the word, "holy"?

What does holiness mean? It doesn't mean spiritual stuffiness. It simply means to be made whole. The bottom line is that sin erodes and destroys. Sin keeps wiping you out, tearing you down. Holiness restores what you were intended to be. That's why the Scripture says the man who fears God and walks in His commandments walks in holiness or wholeness. Holiness leads to happiness. Sin always leads to great sadness and deep sorrow. — Jon Courson, *Jon Courson's Application Commentary: Volume Two: Psalms-Malachi* (Nashville, TN: Thomas Nelson, 2006), 140.

15. Verse 10. What exactly does it mean to fear the Lord?

In addition to praising God for the works He has done, we can praise Him for the wisdom that will come. You see, the fear of the Lord means we are so in love with our Father that we are afraid to do anything that would grieve Him. And it is when we understand this that wisdom truly begins.

When Mary, the sister of Martha and Lazarus, poured costly oil on Jesus, Judas criticized her for being wasteful. Jesus, however commended her for being insightful. "What she has done, she has done for My burial," He said (see John 12:7). The disciples walked with Jesus, ate with Him, and listened to Him. Yet even though He said repeatedly that He was going to Jerusalem to die, His words didn't sink in. Mary understood what the disciples didn't. Why? Because she worshiped Him.

Those who fear the Lord, those who are in awe of Him, those who spend time with Him will have insight and wisdom in a way others won't. May we be those who worship Him. — Jon Courson, *Jon Courson's Application Commentary: Volume Two: Psalms-Malachi* (Nashville, TN: Thomas Nelson, 2006), 140–141.

16. How is life different for those who fear the Lord?

Virtually all of our worry and stress could be alleviated if we understood how to exchange "fear of man" for "fear of the Lord." We need a way to think less often about ourselves and more often about God. "God must be bigger to you than people are," writes Edward Welch in his book, When People are Big and God is Small. When it comes to our family and friends, coworkers and neighbors, our problem is sometimes that we need them (and their approval) for ourselves more than we love them for the glory of God. The task God sets for us in life is to emotionally "require" people less and to love them more.

To escape the fear of man is to recognize that God is the One who is awesome and glorious, not other people. We need to understand and grow in the fear of the Lord— because the person who fears God will fear nothing else! — Joni Eareckson Tada, *Breaking the Bonds of Fear* (Joni Eareckson Tada) (Torrance, CA: Aspire Press, 2012).

17. How can we draw near to a God that we fear?

The fear of the Lord includes a spectrum of attitudes. In one sense, it does indeed mean a terror of God; for we are unclean people who will one day appear before the Almighty, who is holy and morally pure. Such fear shrinks back from God. But for people whose eyes have been opened to God's great love, this terror-fear gradually fades the more we come to know him.

For those who have put their faith in Jesus Christ, fear of the Lord means reverent submission that leads to obedience. Yes, such reverence includes an awareness of our sinfulness and God's holiness, but it is balanced by the knowledge of God's great forgiveness, mercy, and love. A proper fear of the Lord will have us moving from terror, dread, and trembling, toward devotion, adoration, and enjoyment of God. This is the love 1 John 4:18 is speaking of when it says, "There is no fear [terror or dread] in love." — Joni Eareckson Tada, *Breaking the Bonds of Fear* (Joni Eareckson Tada) (Torrance, CA: Aspire Press, 2012).

18. 2 Corinthians 3.17. How does worship change us? (You might look at this in several translations.)

But we all, with unveiled face, beholding as in a mirror the glory of the Lord" (2 Corinthians 3:18). What does it mean to behold the Lord's glory? Paul is speaking here of devoted, focused worship. It is time that is given to God simply to behold Him.

The apostle then quickly adds, "Therefore, since we have this ministry" (4:1). Paul makes it clear that beholding the face of Christ is a ministry we all must devote ourselves to.

The Greek word for beholding in this verse is a very strong expression that indicates not just "taking a look" but "fixing the gaze." It means deciding, "I will not move from this position. Before I try to accomplish a single thing, I must be in God's presence."

Many Christians misinterpret the phrase "beholding as in a mirror" (3:18). They think of a mirror with Jesus' face being reflected back to them. That is not Paul's meaning here. He is speaking of an intensely focused gaze, as if peering at something earnestly through a glass, trying to see it more clearly. We are to "fix our eyes" this way, determined to see God's glory in the face of Christ. We are to shut ourselves in the holy of holies with but one obsession: to gaze so intently, and to commune with such devotion, that we are changed.

The Greek word for changed here is "metamorphosed," meaning "transformed, transfigured." Everyone who goes often into the holy of holies and fixes his gaze intently on Christ is being metamorphosed. A transfiguration is taking place. That person is continually being changed into the likeness and character of Jesus.

Do you see what Paul is saying here? He is telling us, "When you spend time beholding the face of Christ, there is freedom to be changed." This act of submission says, "Lord, my will is Yours. Whatever it takes, transform me into the image of Jesus." — David Wilkerson, *God Is Faithful: A Daily Invitation into the Father Heart of God* (Grand Rapids, MI: Chosen, 2012).

19. **Who will join me in committing to take a walk in a park, or look at the stars, or go to the beach, or do something this week to worship God through the vehicle of nature?**

20. **How can we pray for each other this week?**

Answers, Lesson #3
Does Truth Exist?
John 1.14 – 18; 8.30 – 32; 18.36 - 38
Good Questions Have Groups Talking
www.joshhunt.com

OPEN

Have you read—or listened to—any books on
Apologetics? What have you read that was good?

DIG

1. **Let's begin with Pilate's question in John 18.38. (You might also look at the context, beginning in verse 36.) What is truth?**

   Truth is what corresponds with reality.

2. **At the 2018 Golden Globe awards, Oprah Winfrey famously said that "speaking your truth is the most powerful tool we all have." What do you think she meant by that?**

   Truth is going through a tough time.

   A white woman feels black and represents herself to be so. She rises in the leadership ranks of the NAACP until her fiction is exposed. She refuses to go quietly, however. She feels black, and so she is black.

A 69 year-old man in the Netherlands petitions the court to legally change his age to 49 because that's how he feels.

And, of course, seemingly on a daily basis, men (and more and more boys), with all the chromosomes and body parts that make them distinctly male, declare themselves to be female; and women (and more and more girls) likewise declare themselves to be male. They feel they are one sex or the other; therefore, they are that sex. And we must accept that, regardless of what the truth is.

In a viral video, a 5-foot, 9-inch American Caucasian male asks students at the University of Washington to acknowledge that he's Chinese, or six-foot-five, or a woman. Some hesitate, but no one will tell him what he's saying is not true – that he's not what he says he is. That would be "mean"—and "intolerant."

This "true for you, but not for me" relativism is disconcerting because it requires the acceptance of obvious contradictions, denial of reality, and common sense. Rather than adjusting our lives to the truth, the truth has to adjust itself to us.

But it's very difficult to live this way, not to mention it being highly impractical. We rely on mind-independent universal truths in order to think clearly, to navigate life. Otherwise, we quickly get lost. There must be some things that just are—things that are true. This way points North for everybody, no matter what anyone happens to prefer or sincerely believe.

So, what is truth?

At its root, truth is a match-up with reality. A story, a statement, or belief is only true if it lines up with what's real. It's like a socket wrench fitting perfectly onto a bolt. Reality is the truth-maker; reality makes something true. To say "the earth is flat" or "the moon is made of green cheese" is false. Why? Because it doesn't match up with reality.

Until quite recently, the purpose of all education in large part was the pursuit of truth. The motto of Harvard University, for example, is "veritas," Latin for "truth."

No more. Anyone who says education should be about the pursuit of truth is immediately shot down with the comeback: "Whose truth?"

Increasingly, people speak of "my truth," or say "it's true for me," or "your reality"—as though truth is merely a matter of opinion or perspective. At the 2018 Golden Globe awards, Oprah Winfrey famously said that "speaking your truth is the most powerful tool we all have." https://www.prageru.com/video/true-for-you-but-not-for-me/

3. What is wrong with this picture of truth?

Now, you can have your experience or your perspective. But there is no such thing as "your truth" or "my truth." There is only the truth—that which is true for everyone.

As Wall Street Journal writer Byron Tau noted, "Oprah employed a phrase that I've noticed a lot of other celebrities using these days: 'your truth' instead of 'the truth.'" But, he added, "'your truth' undermines the idea of shared common facts."

And here's another problem with "your truth": If "your truth" is truth, anyone who doesn't hold that truth must be wrong. This sounds a lot like narcissism. And it's intellectual bullying. "Believe 'my truth'—or else." Not exactly a positive, pro-truth message.

Yeah, truth is going through a tough time.

So let's review: Truth can't be relative. If it is relative, it's not truth. To say "there is no truth for all people" is to declare a truth for all people. In effect, you're saying, "It's true that there is no truth!" And to declare that both your and my opinions are true even if they contradict one another is to speak nonsense.

Truth isn't opinion or preference. It's not subjective or relative. It is inescapable because reality is inescapable.

No amount of double-talk will change that.

And that's the truth. https://www.prageru.com/video/true-for-you-but-not-for-me/

4. John 1.14 – 18. What do we learn about truth from this passage?

THE passage of Scripture now before us is very short, if we measure it by words. But it is very long, if we measure it by the nature of its contents. The substance of it is so immensely important that we shall do well to give it separate and distinct consideration. This single verse contains more than enough matter for a whole exposition.

The main truth which this verse teaches is the reality of our Lord Jesus Christ's incarnation, or being made man. St. John tells us that "the Word was made flesh, and dwelt among us."

The plain meaning of these words is, that our divine Saviour really took human nature upon Him, in order to save sinners. He really became a man like ourselves in all things, sin only excepted. Like ourselves, he was born of a woman, though born in a miraculous manner. Like ourselves, He grew from infancy to boyhood, and from boyhood to man's estate, both in wisdom and in stature. (Luke 2:52.) Like ourselves, he hungered, thirsted, ate, drank, slept, was wearied, felt pain, wept, rejoiced, marvelled, was moved to anger and compassion. Having be come flesh, and taken a body, He prayed, read the Scriptures, suffered being tempted, and submitted His human will to the will of God the Father. And finally, in the same body, He really suffered and shed His blood, really died, was really buried, really rose again, and really ascended up into heaven. And yet all this time He was God as well as man! — J. C. Ryle, *Expository Thoughts on John, vol. 1* (New York: Robert Carter & Brothers, 1879), 24–25.

5. What do we learn about Jesus from this passage?

This union of two natures in Christ's one Person is doubtless one of the greatest mysteries of the Christian religion. It needs to be carefully stated. It is just one of those great truths which are not meant to be curiously pried into, but to be reverently believed. Nowhere, perhaps, shall we find a more wise and judicious statement than in the second article of the Church of England. "The Son, which is the Word of the Father, begotten from everlasting of the Father, the very and eternal God, and of one substance with the Father, took man's nature in the womb of the blessed Virgin of her substance: so that two whole and perfect natures, that is to say, the Godhead and the manhood, were joined together in one Person, never to be divided, whereof is one Christ, very God and very man." This is a most valuable declaration. This is "sound speech, which cannot be condemned." — J. C. Ryle, *Expository*

Thoughts on John, vol. 1 (New York: Robert Carter & Brothers, 1879), 25.

6. The Word (God) became flesh. Did the Word quit being God?

But while we do not pretend to explain the union of two natures in our Lord Jesus Christ's Person, we must not hesitate to fence the subject with well-defined cautions. While we state most carefully what we do believe, we must not shrink from declaring boldly what we do not believe. We must never forget, that though our Lord was God and man at the same time, the divine and human natures in Him were never confounded. One nature did not swallow up the other. The two natures remained perfect and distinct. The divinity of Christ was never for a moment laid aside, although veiled. The manhood of Christ, during His life-time, was never for a moment unlike our own, though by union with the Godhead, greatly dignified. Though perfect God, Christ has always been perfect man from the first moment of His incarnation. He that is gone into heaven, and is sitting at the Father's right hand to intercede for sinners, is man as well as God. Though perfect man, Christ never ceased to be perfect God. He that suffered for sin on the cross, and was made sin for us, was "God manifest in the flesh." The blood with which the Church was purchased, is called the blood "of God." (Acts 20:28.) Though He became "flesh" in the fullest sense, when He was born of the Virgin Mary, He never at any period ceased to be the Eternal Word. To say that He constantly manifested His divine nature during His earthly ministry, would, of course, be contrary to plain facts. To attempt to explain why His Godhead was sometimes veiled and at other times unveiled, while He was on earth, would be venturing on ground which we had better leave alone. But to say that at any instant of His earthly ministry

He was not fully and entirely God, is nothing less than heresy. — J. C. Ryle, *Expository Thoughts on John, vol. 1* (New York: Robert Carter & Brothers, 1879), 25–26.

7. How much difference does it make that we get this doctrine right? How big of a deal is this?

The cautions just given may seem at first sight needless, wearisome, and hair-splitting. It is precisely the neglect of such cautions which ruins many souls. This constant undivided union of two perfect natures in Christ's Person is exactly that which gives infinite value to His mediation, and qualifies Him to be the very Mediator that sinners need. Our Mediator is One who can sympathize with us, because He is very man. And yet, at the same time, He is One who can deal with the Father for us on equal terms, because He is very God.—It is the same union which gives infinite value to His righteousness, when imputed to believers. It is the righteousness of One who was God as well as man.—It is the same union which gives infinite value to the atoning blood which He shed for sinners on the cross. It is the blood of One who was God as well as man.—It is the same union which gives infinite value to His resurrection. When He rose again, as the Head of the body of believers, He rose not as a mere man, but as God.—Let these things sink deeply into our hearts. The second Adam is far greater than the first Adam was. The first Adam was only man, and so he fell. The second Adam was God as well as man, and so He completely conquered. — J. C. Ryle, *Expository Thoughts on John, vol. 1* (New York: Robert Carter & Brothers, 1879), 26–27.

8. The Word became flesh. What difference does it make? What are the implications.

Let us leave the subject with feelings of deep gratitude and thankfulness. It is full of abounding consolation for all who know Christ by faith, and believe on Him.

Did the Word become flesh? Then He is One who can be touched with the feeling of His people's infirmities, because He has suffered Himself, being tempted. He is almighty because He is God, and yet He can feel with us, because He is man.

Did the Word become flesh? Then He can supply us with a perfect pattern and example for our daily life. Had he walked among us as an angel or a spirit, we could never have copied Him. But having dwelt among us as a man, we know that the true standard of holiness is to "walk even as He walked." (1 John 2:6.) He is a perfect pattern, because He is God. But He is also a pattern exactly suited to our wants, because He is man.

Finally, did the Word become flesh? Then let us see in our mortal bodies a real, true dignity, and not defile them by sin. Vile and weak as our body may seem, it is a body which the Eternal Son of God was not ashamed to take upon Himself, and to take up to heaven. That simple fact is a pledge that He will raise our bodies at the last day, and glorify them together with His own. — J. C. Ryle, *Expository Thoughts on John, vol. 1* (New York: Robert Carter & Brothers, 1879), 27–28.

9. Jesus was full of grace and truth. Does that suggest we need to balance grace with truth?

Does the Bible teach a balance between grace and truth as though the two are separate realities? It does not. To the contrary, Scripture inseparably joins the two together in the person of Jesus Christ. The Bible says, "The Law was given through Moses; grace and truth were realized through Jesus Christ" (John 1:17).

John says here that grace and truth came to fullness (to fruition) in the person of Jesus Christ. He wasn't part grace and part truth. He was 100 percent grace and 100 percent truth! You can find the qualities of both in Christ. They're in perfect harmony and unity. All by itself, John 1:17 proves that grace and truth are not opposed to one another.

If you're going to draw a line, draw it between grace and legalism—not between grace and truth. The Bible plainly puts grace and truth on the same side of the line, in Jesus. So anytime you hear people say, "Well, this message of grace is good, but you have to balance that with truth," you can recognize what they are doing. Whether they are sincerely mistaken or committed legalists, you can know that it's a lie, because grace and truth are not on two different sides of the dividing line. They're on the same side of the line. Legalism is on the other side of the line. Grace and truth are synonymous because they are expressed (or personified) in the person of Jesus Christ, who is "full of grace and truth."

Why do we struggle so much with this? Admittedly, human beings often aren't in balance. We do tend to lean toward different extremes. But let's not confuse this matter of grace and truth. Grace and truth are in perfect harmony. There's nothing to balance between them. They're perfectly complementary. — Steve McVey, *52 Lies Heard in Church Every Sunday: ...and Why the Truth Is so Much Better* (Eugene, OR: Harvest House Publishers, 2011).

10. What problems does balancing grace with truth create?

The lie that we need to find a balance between grace and truth might sound good to those who don't know better, but I can't overstate the devastating effect of attempting to divide the two. Grace and truth are conjoined twins. You cannot separate them without killing both.

To suggest that we should find balance within the topic of grace is an insidious lie. Any attempt to do that is to compromise grace. Grace is Jesus, and He doesn't need to be balanced with anything. Balance Him with truth? Reject that nonsense. He is truth!

Whether they know it or not, people who say that we need to maintain a balance in the teaching of grace are suggesting that it needs to be watered down so that it's not so offensive to the legalist. Remember, the legalist feels like there must be something that we have to contribute to this life we have received in Christ. But as we've discussed, you can't add anything. You already have Jesus, and He is grace and truth—the whole truth and nothing but the truth. — Steve McVey, *52 Lies Heard in Church Every Sunday: ...and Why the Truth Is so Much Better* (Eugene, OR: Harvest House Publishers, 2011).

11. John 8.30 – 32. What do we learn about discipleship from this passage?

A disciple is one who continues in God's Word. Jesus said, "If ye continue in [studying, practicing] my word, then are ye my disciples indeed" (John 8:31). True disciples persevere in the Word. They are deeply serious, irrevocably committed, student-followers of the Son of God, ever seeking more of Him—more study, more obedience, more conformity to His image. Christians who start studying and obeying, but due to offenses, adversities, prosperity, or other interests stop, forfeit discipleship.

A disciple is a person of truth. Jesus added, "Ye [disciples] shall know the truth" (v. 32). Disciples love truth in all forms. They love the Bible, the sole standard of spiritual truth. They love honesty, or truthfulness of heart and speech. They love fidelity, or faithfulness in all dealings. And they love reality, preferring facing actual conditions to trusting in illusions. Christians who prefer dishonesty, unfaithfulness, unreality, or un- or extrabiblical teachings can't be disciples. — Greg Hinnant, *Not by Bread Alone: Daily Devotions for Disciples* (Lake Mary, FL: Creation House, 2012).

12. What does it mean that the truth will set you free?

We don't always want to face truth because sometimes it is painful. Sometimes it shows us that we need to change. If we are behaving badly, we make excuses for our wrong behavior. But excuses will never make us free. Let God get involved with your day; when you feel your temper flare, ask Him to reveal the truth of that situation. The truth will always set you free to enjoy the rest of your day. — Joyce Meyer, *Starting Your Day Right: Devotions for Each Morning of the Year* (New York City, NY: FaithWords, 2004).

13. What does it mean to know the truth?

The foremost problem with this statement is in what it leaves out. To suggest that the truth will set you free is only a partial quote from Jesus Himself. What He actually said, in its totality, is this: "You will know the truth, and the truth will set you free."

Biblical truth alone has no ability to bring about any change in our lives. The Pharisees proved that. Although they knew their Bibles as well as anybody in their day, their knowledge of biblical content did nothing for them. To them, Bible study was an end unto itself. In other words, they studied the Bible to know the Bible. As strange as it may seem, that is a terrible reason to study Scripture. In fact, it can make a modern-day Pharisee out of you!

We don't study the Bible to learn its contents. We study the Bible to know its Author. It is only as the Scripture leads us into an experiential knowledge of our God that it has fulfilled its purpose in our lives. Remember that Jesus told the Pharisees concerning the Scriptures, "These are they which testify of Me" (John 5:39 NKJV). If you've found something other than Jesus Christ through Bible study, you've missed the point. Again, we don't study the Bible in order to learn it. We study it to learn Him. — Steve McVey, *52 Lies Heard in Church Every Sunday: ...and Why the Truth Is so Much Better* (Eugene, OR: Harvest House Publishers, 2011).

14. What is the difference between knowing the truth and knowing about the truth?

The modern church world has taken the idea that the truth will set you free and has mistakenly believed that learning the propositional truths of Scripture will change us. Because of that viewpoint, they've turned the Bible into a handbook of religious guidelines. Ask them if the Bible is a book of guidelines for life, and most will say no. They profess to have a higher view of Scripture than that, but watch the way the application of Scripture to people's lives is made in sermons and Bible studies, and you'll come to a different conclusion about what they really believe.

There is often much application about what we are to now do that mentions nothing about knowing our Savior more intimately. Some may call this sort of teaching practical, but I think a better term for it could be Christianity Lite because its emphasis is so heavy on religious performance and so light on Christ Himself.

Unless they find a biblical principle of some sort and then show how that principle should guide our actions, many people think the teaching isn't practical. In reality, the demand for "practical teaching" in the church world today is a subtle mask for an underlying hunger to be doing something as opposed to knowing Someone. Certainly, nothing is wrong with understanding the practical ways that Christ wants to express Himself through our daily lifestyle. But people often teach biblical principles in such a way as to suggest that the aim of Christian living is to do right things. And nothing could be further from the truth. Remember, it's about knowing Him. All the doing will flow from that. When we reverse the two, we end up with nothing more than dead religious works, regardless of how admirable they may look to everybody around us. — Steve McVey, *52 Lies Heard in Church Every Sunday: ...and Why the Truth Is so Much Better* (Eugene, OR: Harvest House Publishers, 2011).

15. Steve McVey says, "We have not been called to live by biblical truths." What in the world do you think he meant by that? Do you agree?

We have not been called to live by biblical truths. We have been called to live by the truth, who is the indwelling Christ. He is our life source, and He animates our daily actions, not religious determination to act on information we might have learned. After I have shared a message from the Bible that focuses on Jesus Christ, sometimes somebody tells me that they wished the message had been more practical. When this happens, I inwardly shudder. Where did we ever get the idea that telling people what to do is a better way to teach the Bible than showing them who their God is? Jesus came to reveal the Father to us, not to tell us how to live. If that was His purpose in the world, doesn't it seem reasonable to argue that it's a good purpose statement for those who profess to follow Him?

Many people think that if we build our lives around biblical principles, then we'll experience the life God intends for us. As a result, we design a multitude of religious programs to help us learn the content of the Bible. We are largely a generation of Christians who think that the better we learn the Bible, the better life will be. "Christian education" has become a matter of memorizing Scripture at the novice end of the spectrum and parsing Greek verbs at the advanced end. But if that's the only thing that has happened, the result is a person who has some degree of Bible education but still hasn't been set free to really live. Studying the Bible is not enough. We must engage with the Spirit of Christ through the Scripture to find real freedom.

The ultimate truth of the Bible is Christ Jesus. He said, "I am...the truth" (John 14:6). Knowing biblical content can actually be harmful if it doesn't strengthen our knowledge of Jesus. Paul wrote that "knowledge puffs up" (1 Corinthians 8:1). It leads to arrogance rather than love. — Steve McVey, *52 Lies Heard in Church Every Sunday: ...and Why the Truth Is so Much Better* (Eugene, OR: Harvest House Publishers, 2011).

16. This may again sound like theological hair splitting. What practical difference does it make?

The Truth Is So Much Better!

Jesus said, "I am the way, and the truth, and the life" (John 14:6). He is the One who sets us free. Biblical truth points us to the ultimate truth, which is Him. He alone is the One who can free us to live the life our creator intends for us to enjoy. That life flows from the union we share with our triune God. Jesus is "the way" we are to enjoy "the life" by living experientially in "the truth," which means to consciously live with the knowledge that He is our very life source.

Substituting truth with a small t for Jesus Christ is to take teachings of the Bible and try to apply them to our lives as a moral compass for our behavior. If unbelievers say they like Jesus but only apply the moral teachings He gives to their lives, we often see the folly in such an approach. But the same is true when believers approach the Bible that way. It is only when we encounter the Truth with a capital T (which is Jesus Christ Himself) that we will know Him firsthand. Only then does the truth transform us and set us free.

When Jesus said, "You shall know the truth and the truth shall set you free," He used the Greek word ginōskō. It is the same word used in Matthew 1:25 when the Bible says that Joseph "knew her [Mary] not till she had brought forth her firstborn son" (KJV).

Obviously, Joseph was acquainted with Mary before Jesus was born. The word knew means much more than that in the verse. The word was used as a Jewish idiom for physical intimacy with another person. It's interesting that Jesus used the same word when He spoke of knowing the truth that the Bible uses about Joseph and his intimate relationship to Mary. Jesus was indicating that truth alone will not set you free, but it is by an intimate knowledge of the truth that we are set free. — Steve McVey, *52 Lies Heard in Church Every*

Sunday: ...and Why the Truth Is so Much Better (Eugene, OR: Harvest House Publishers, 2011).

17. John 8.31. What does it mean to hold to Jesus' teachings? You might check more than one translation.

According to Jesus, a single condition demonstrates the truth of our discipleship: "If you abide in my word" (John 8:31). It is not enough to have warm feelings toward Jesus or to find some of his teachings agreeable. We are reminded again, having seen this many times in John's Gospel, that Jesus is not interested in gathering large numbers of loosely committed admirers. Instead, he seeks and calls for true disciples, that is, those who abide in his Word.

The word abide is a significant one in the Gospel of John, especially in Jesus' teaching on the vine and the branches in chapter 15. The ordinary meaning of abide is to "remain," "continue," or "dwell." But Jesus also has in mind the idea of a life connection. He said, "I am the true vine.... Abide in me, and I in you. As the branch cannot bear fruit by itself, unless it abides in the vine, neither can you, unless you abide in me" (John 15:1–4). Jesus' concern, therefore, is not merely that we should continue to call ourselves Christians, but that we should abide in his Word in the way that a branch abides in the vine. The branch receives its life from the vine and bears the fruit of the vine. Likewise, Jesus teaches, true disciples are those who find their life in his Word and in that way bear his fruit. Again, linking this abiding to true discipleship, Jesus said, "By this my Father is glorified, that you bear much fruit and so prove to be my disciples" (15:8). — Richard D. Phillips, *John*, ed. Richard D. Phillips, Philip Graham Ryken, and Daniel M.

Doriani, *1st ed., vol. 1, Reformed Expository Commentary* (Phillipsburg, NJ: P&R Publishing, 2014), 539.

18. If you hold to my teaching. What is the application?

True faith in Jesus receives salvation immediately— anyone who truly believes in Jesus is forgiven of his sins and justified before God on the spot. But the truth of our faith—its validity—is proved only as we continue and abide in the life and Word of Jesus. It is in this sense that abiding is the condition of true discipleship. In John's Gospel, we encounter many who come to Jesus with a fickle faith. In fact, these "believers" of John 8 are mainly composed of such false converts. Before the chapter is over, most of those who "believed" are picking up stones to throw at him (John 8:59). But Jesus seeks and approves only a faith that demonstrates its truth by abiding in him.

This calls for a serious point of application. Ours is a day in which the "faith" of many so-called Christians consists mainly of verbal assent. We respond positively to Jesus and perhaps delight in his promises. But are you abiding in his Word? Is the Word of God the food for your soul in which you constantly abide? Is your "faith" in Jesus high enough among your priorities that you devote yourself to serious Bible study? And is the Word of God increasingly manifesting godly fruit in your life? Is your character changing? Are your habits being reformed? Has your attitude toward time, relationships, money, and speech been molded by the teaching of Jesus and the prophets and apostles who have written on his behalf? If the answer is "No," then you have real cause to question the reality of your faith. If the answer is "It's hard to tell," then you also have cause for alarm. "If you abide in my word," Jesus insists, "you are truly my disciples" (John 8:31).

Jesus once told a parable that illustrated the difference between the two kinds of "faith." He described four kinds of soil on which the seed of God's Word falls. The first three depict people who are shown not to be his true disciples. The first was a hard path, and the seed lay there until it was taken away by birds. This depicts the open unbeliever, who neither understands nor accepts God's Word. The second soil was "rocky ground, where they did not have much soil." In that case, the seed quickly sprang up, "but when the sun rose they were scorched. And since they had no root, they withered away" (Matt. 13:5–6). This depicts those who receive the gospel with joy, but in whom the truth of Christ does not penetrate deeply. The result is that "when tribulation or persecution arises on account of the word," such people fall away from following Christ (13:21). The third soil was infested with weeds and thorns. "This is the one who hears the word, but the cares of the world and the deceitfulness of riches choke the word, and it proves unfruitful" (13:22). — Richard D. Phillips, *John*, ed. Richard D. Phillips, Philip Graham Ryken, and Daniel M. Doriani, *1st ed., vol. 1, Reformed Expository Commentary* (Phillipsburg, NJ: P&R Publishing, 2014), 539–540.

19. Summary. What did you learn today? What do you want to remember and apply?

20. How can we pray for each other this week?

Answers, Lesson #4
Is Jesus God? / Luke 1.26 - 35
Good Questions Have Groups Talking
www.joshhunt.com

OPEN

What are your plans for Christmas?

DIG

1. **Luke 1.26 – 35. As we read this passage, look for anything that you have never noticed before.**

   We should notice, in the first place, the lowly and unassuming manner in which the Saviour of mankind came amongst us. The angel who announced His advent, was sent to an obscure town of Galilee, named Nazareth. The woman who was honored to be our Lord's mother, was evidently in a humble position of life. Both in her station and her dwelling-place, there was an utter absence of what the world calls "greatness."

   We need not hesitate to conclude, that there was a wise providence in all this arrangement. The Almighty counsel, which orders all things in heaven and earth, could just as easily have appointed Jerusalem to be the place of Mary's residence as Nazareth, or could as easily have chosen the daughter of some rich scribe to be our Lord's mother, as a poor woman. But it seemed good that it should not be so. The first advent of Messiah was to be an advent of humiliation. That humiliation was to begin even from the time of His conception and birth. — J. C. Ryle, *Expository Thoughts on Luke, vol. 1* (New York: Robert Carter & Brothers, 1879), 21–22.

2. **We always want to read the Bible for application. We want to be doers of the Word. What application do you find in this passage?**

Let us beware of despising poverty in others, and of being ashamed of it if God lays it upon ourselves. The condition of life which Jesus voluntarily chose, ought always to be regarded with holy reverence. The common tendency of the day to bow down before rich men, and make an idol of money, ought to be carefully resisted and discouraged. The example of our Lord is a sufficient answer to a thousand grovelling maxims about wealth, which pass current among men. "Though He was rich, yet for our sakes He became poor." (2 Cor. 8:9.) — J. C. Ryle, *Expository Thoughts on Luke, vol. 1* (New York: Robert Carter & Brothers, 1879), 22.

3. **What do we learn about Jesus from this story?**

Let us admire the amazing condescension of the Son of God. The Heir of all things not only took our nature upon Him, but took it in the most humbling form in which it could have been assumed. It would have been condescension to come on earth as a king and reign. It was a miracle of mercy passing our comprehension to come on earth as a poor man, to be despised, and suffer, and die. Let His love constrain us to live not to ourselves, but to Him. Let His example daily bring home to our conscience the precept of Scripture: "Mind not high things, but condescend to men of low estate." (Rom. 12:16.) — J. C. Ryle, *Expository Thoughts on Luke, vol. 1* (New York: Robert Carter & Brothers, 1879), 22.

4. What do we learn about Mary?

We should notice, in the second place, the high privilege of the Virgin Mary. The language which the angel Gabriel addresses to her is very remarkable. He calls her "highly favored." He tells her that "the Lord is with her." He says to her, "Blessed art thou among women." — J. C. Ryle, *Expository Thoughts on Luke, vol. 1* (New York: Robert Carter & Brothers, 1879), 22.

5. In theology, we have categories. Soteriology is the study of salvation. Eschatology is the study of last things. Ecclesiology is the study of the church. Catholics have a category in theology called Mariology. How do Catholics think of Mary differently than we do?

It is a well-known fact, that the Roman Catholic Church pays an honor to the Virgin Mary, hardly inferior to that which it pays to her blessed Son. She is formally declared by the Roman Catholic Church to have been "conceived without sin." She is held up to Roman Catholics as an object of worship, and prayed to as a mediator between God and man, no less powerful than Christ Himself. For all this, be it remembered, there is not the slightest warrant in Scripture. There is no warrant in the verses before us now. There is no warrant in any other part of God's word.

But while we say this, we must in fairness admit, that no woman was ever so highly honored as the mother of our Lord. It is evident that one woman only out of the countless millions of the human race, could be the means whereby God could be "manifest in the flesh," and the Virgin Mary had the mighty privilege of being that one. By one woman, sin and death were brought into the world at the beginning. By the child-bearing of one woman, life and immortality were brought to light when Christ was born. No wonder that this one woman was called "highly favored" and "dlessed."

One thing in connexion with this subject should never be forgotten by Christians. There is a relationship to Christ within reach of us all,—a relationship far nearer than that of flesh and blood,—a relationship which belongs to all who repent and believe. "Whosoever shall do the will of God," says Jesus, "the same is my brother, and sister, and mother."—"Blessed is the womb that bare thee," was the saying of a woman one day. But what was the reply? "Yea! rather blessed are they that hear the word of God and keep it." (Mark 3:35; Luke 11:27.) — J. C. Ryle, *Expository Thoughts on Luke, vol. 1* (New York: Robert Carter & Brothers, 1879), 23–24.

6. What do Catholics get wrong in their Mariology?

The angel's greeting has often been misunderstood. Gabriel was not worshiping Mary; nor did he say that she was "full of grace." These ideas come from a prayer commonly used by Roman Catholics: "Hail Mary, full of grace; the Lord is with thee. Blessed art thou among women, and blessed is the fruit of thy womb, Jesus, Holy Mary, Mother of God, pray for us sinners now and at the hour of death." This is not a biblical prayer, although it has some biblical language in it. The problem is that it treats Mary as the source of grace rather than as an object of grace. People pray to Mary because they think she has grace to give. But the phrase "full of grace" is based on a Latin translation (the Vulgate) that is really a mistranslation. Even Roman Catholic Bible scholars admit this, although most still think that Christians should pray to Mary.[6] What the Bible actually says is that Mary was the recipient of God's grace, not a repository of grace. The word that the English Standard Version rightly translates as "favored one" is a passive participle. In other words, it refers to the grace that Mary was given by God, and not to any grace that she can give to others.

It is important to know what to believe about Mary because so many people go wrong at this point. The Bible never says that Mary was without sin, that she remained a virgin, or that she is able to give grace to sinners. We can only imagine how much it would grieve her to know that some people worship her! What the Bible does say—beyond the fact that she was the mother of Jesus—is that she was saved by grace. The way Mary helps us is not by giving us grace, but by showing that God can give us the same kind of grace that he gave to her. Mary is the blessed virgin, who alone was called to give birth to the Son of God. Her experience is not our experience; nevertheless, her example is for us. Since she received grace from God, her example proves that God shows unmerited favor to lowly sinners. Even when we feel small and insignificant, overlooked by the world, we can know that God is for us. Gabriel's greeting shows God's grace for the lowly.
— Philip Graham Ryken, *Luke*, ed. Richard D. Phillips, Philip Graham Ryken, and Daniel M. Doriani, *vol. 1, Reformed Expository Commentary* (Phillipsburg, NJ: P&R Publishing, 2009), 30–31.

7. What do we learn about God from the story of Mary?

It is doubtful whether Gabriel could have found a more unlikely person to greet anywhere in Israel. Mary was among the lowly. She was young—possibly as young as twelve or thirteen years old, in that awkward stage between childhood and womanhood.2 Like many people in Israel, she was a poor, uneducated peasant living in a small country town far from the center of power. As people said in those days, "Can anything good come out of Nazareth?" (John 1:46). Mary was also a female in a culture that discounted women. From a merely human perspective, she was insignificant. Kent Hughes calls her "a nobody in a nothing town in the middle of nowhere."3

Yet Mary was given the greatest honor that any woman has ever been given. She was chosen to be the mother of Jesus, and her lowly estate was part of God's plan. By choosing Mary, God was beginning to show what humiliation his Son would have to endure for the salvation of sinners. Martin Luther observed that God might well "have gone to Jerusalem and picked out Caiaphas's daughter, who was fair, rich, clad in gold embroidered raiment and attended by a retinue of maids in waiting. But God preferred a lowly maid from a mean town."4 God preferred this because the plan of salvation required Jesus to humble himself, and only then to be exalted. To rescue us from our sins and lift us to glory, Jesus first had to enter into the misery of our lost and fallen condition. What better way to show what he had come to do than for him to be born to a woman like Mary from a town like Nazareth?

God's grace is for the lowly. God certainly showed grace to Mary. This is the meaning of the angel's salutation: "Greetings, O favored one, the Lord is with you!" (Luke 1:28). With these words, Gabriel pronounced God's benediction on Mary. God was with her to bless her, not because of her own merit, but because of his grace. The word the angel used for "favor" (kecharitōmenē) comes from the Greek word for "grace" (charis). It means to be treated with undeserved kindness. Martin Luther paraphrased Gabriel's greeting like this: "O Mary, you are blessed. You have a gracious God. No woman has ever lived on earth to whom God has shown such grace."

— Philip Graham Ryken, *Luke*, ed. Richard D. Phillips, Philip Graham Ryken, and Daniel M. Doriani, *vol. 1, Reformed Expository Commentary* (Phillipsburg, NJ: P&R Publishing, 2009), 29–30.

8. Read for emotion. How did this event feel to Mary? Put yourself in her shoes.

What the angel said was meant to be reassuring, yet Mary was still troubled. She wasn't hysterical, as some teenagers might have been, but she was more than a little upset. As Luke tells it, "She was greatly troubled at the saying, and tried to discern what sort of greeting this might be" (Luke 1:29). Naturally Mary wanted to know what this meant. What was happening? Why was an angel talking to her? What had he come to say?

Gabriel did not leave Mary in suspense, but followed his greeting with an announcement. The announcement— which came in two parts because it was divided by Mary's question in verse 34—began as follows: "Do not be afraid, Mary, for you have found favor with God. And behold, you will conceive in your womb and bear a son, and you shall call his name Jesus. He will be great and will be called the Son of the Most High. And the Lord God will give to him the throne of his father David, and he will reign over the house of Jacob forever, and of his kingdom there will be no end" (Luke 1:30–33).
— Philip Graham Ryken, *Luke*, ed. Richard D. Phillips, Philip Graham Ryken, and Daniel M. Doriani, *vol. 1, Reformed Expository Commentary* (Phillipsburg, NJ: P&R Publishing, 2009), 31–32.

9. **Mary was highly favored. She is, perhaps, the most famous, most loved and admired woman in history. Was hers and easy life or a hard life?**

Mary was not called to an easy task, for she would be misunderstood and would endure much personal sorrow (2:34–35). But God's grace would always be available and adequate. The word translated "highly favored" in Luke 1:28 is applied to all believers in Ephesians 1:6 and translated "his glorious grace, which he has freely given us in the One he loves." God's abundant grace is available to us just as it was to Mary! Why should we be afraid? — David W. Wiersbe and Warren W. Wiersbe, *C Is for Christmas: The History, Personalities, and Meaning of Christ's Birth: An A to Z Guide* (Grand Rapids, MI: Baker Books, 2012), 64.

10. **Luke 1.26. Pledged. How does your translation have it? What was the relationship between Mary and Joseph?**

According to Jewish custom, based upon the arrangement made between their parents, a couple could become engaged even as young children. Then, a year before their marriage, they would become espoused, which meant that although they would not consummate their relationship, they would be considered husband and wife in a legal binding so strong, it required a divorce to break the relationship. — Jon Courson, *Jon Courson's Application Commentary* (Nashville, TN: Thomas Nelson, 2003), 297.

11. **What do John's birth, and Jesus' birth have in common?**

John came first. He was the forerunner—the messenger sent ahead to announce the coming of the King. Then came Jesus—his Majesty, the King—to seek and to save the lost. In the opening chapters of Luke their stories are laid out side by side for comparison and contrast. John and Jesus: two cousins, two pregnancies, two hymns of praise, and two deliveries at the beginning of two great lives.

The similarities between the two stories are striking. Both John and Jesus were born to godly women who apart from divine intervention were unable to bear children. Writing in the fourth century, Maximus of Turin described how "Mary, conscious of her virginity, marvels at the fruit hidden in her belly, while Elizabeth, conscious of her old age, blushes that her womb is heavy with the one she has conceived."1 The births of both cousins were announced by the same awesome angel, who told people not to be afraid, proclaimed the birth of a son, gave each child his name, and explained his mission in life. The people who heard these announcements— Zechariah the priest and Mary the virgin—questioned the angel and were given a confirming sign. — Philip Graham Ryken, *Luke*, ed. Richard D. Phillips, Philip Graham Ryken, and Daniel M. Doriani, *vol. 1, Reformed Expository Commentary* (Phillipsburg, NJ: P&R Publishing, 2009), 28–29.

12. What do they NOT have in common?

Yet for all their similarities, what Luke mainly wants us to see are the differences. Like a white paint chip next to an off-white paint chip, the comparison is made to show the contrast. So who is greater: John or Jesus? John's mother was barren; the mother of Jesus had never been with a man at all. John would be a prophet crying in the wilderness; Jesus would reign on David's everlasting throne. John would be "great before the Lord" (Luke 1:15). Jesus would be "great" without qualification (Luke 1:32), the Son of the Most High God. John would be filled with the Holy Spirit, but Jesus would be conceived by the Holy Spirit. John would prepare for God's coming, but when Jesus came, God was there, in the flesh. Who is greater: John or Jesus? Luke argues from the lesser to the greater to give more glory to Jesus. Jesus was like John, but superior in every respect—infinitely superior. — Philip Graham Ryken, *Luke*, ed. Richard D. Phillips, Philip Graham Ryken, and Daniel M. Doriani, *vol. 1, Reformed Expository Commentary* (Phillipsburg, NJ: P&R Publishing, 2009), 29.

13. Luke 1.27. How important is the doctrine of the Virgin Birth? What would change if this were left out?

The virgin birth is an underlying assumption in everything the Bible says about Jesus. To throw out the virgin birth is to reject Christ's deity, the accuracy and authority of Scripture, and a host of other related doctrines that are the heart of the Christian faith. No issue is more important than the virgin birth to our understanding of who Jesus is. If we deny that Jesus is God, we have denied the very essence of Christianity. Everything else the Bible teaches about Christ hinges on the truth we celebrate at Christmas—that Jesus is God in human flesh. If the story of His birth is merely a fabricated or trumped–up legend, then so is the rest of what Scripture tells us about Him. The virgin birth is as crucial as the resurrection in substantiating His deity. It is not an optional truth. Anyone who rejects Christ's deity rejects Christ absolutely—even if he pretends otherwise (see 1 John 4:1–3). — John MacArthur, *Truth for Today : A Daily Touch of God's Grace* (Nashville, Tenn.: J. Countryman, 2001), 382.

14. Luke 1.31. What does the name "Jesus" mean?

Mary is told that she will have a son and that she is to give him the name Jesus (v. 31, a name which originally meant, "Lord, help!" but had come to be understood as meaning "salvation"; see Matt. 1:21). — Craig A. Evans, *Luke, Understanding the Bible Commentary Series* (Grand Rapids, MI: Baker Books, 1990), 25.

15. Luke 1.33. Kingdom. This is a key word in the gospels. What exactly is the kingdom of God?

This vision of the kingdom is where Jesus started and where we must also start. He came announcing, manifesting, and teaching the availability and nature of the kingdom of the heavens. "For I was sent for this purpose," he said (Luke 4:43).

The kingdom of God is the range of God's effective will, where what God wants done is done.3 Earth and its immediate surroundings seem to be the only place in creation where God permits his will to not be done. Therefore we pray, "Thy kingdom come, Thy will be done in earth, as it is in heaven" (Matthew 6:10, KJV) and hope for the time when that kingdom will be completely fulfilled even here on earth, where, in fact, it is already present (see Luke 17:21) and available to those who seek it with all their heart (see Matthew 6:33; 11:12; Luke 16:16). For those who seek it, it is true even now that all things work together for their good and that nothing can cut them off from God's inseparable love and effective care (see Romans 8:28, 35–39).

The vision that underlies spiritual transformation into Christlikeness is, then, the vision of life now and forever in the range of God's effective will, that is, partaking of the divine nature through a birth "from above" and participating by our actions in what God is doing now in our lifetime on earth (see 2 Peter 1:4, 1 John 3:1–2). Therefore, we can say, "Whatever we do, speaking or acting, we do all on behalf of the Lord Jesus, giving thanks through him to God the Father" (Colossians 3:17, PAR). In everything we do, we are permitted to do his work. What we are aiming for in this vision is to live fully in the kingdom of God, as fully as possible now and here, not just hereafter. — Dallas Willard and Jan Johnson, *Renovation of the Heart in Daily Practice: Experiments in Spiritual Transformation* (Colorado Springs, CO: NavPress, 2006), 57–58.

16. What is life like in the Kingdom of God?

Every time you are in conflict with someone, when you want to hurt them, gossip about them, avoid them, but instead you go to them and seek reconciliation and forgiveness, the Kingdom is breaking into this world.

Every time you have a chunk of money and you decide to give sacrificially to somebody who is hungry or homeless or poor, the Kingdom is breaking into the world.

Every time somebody who has an addiction wants to partner with God so badly that they're willing to stop hiding, acknowledge the truth, and get help from a loving community, the Kingdom is breaking into the world.

Every time a workaholic parent decides to stop idolizing their job and rearranges their life to begin to love and care for the little children entrusted to them, the Kingdom is breaking into the world.

This good news happens through Jesus. Jesus himself— through his incarnation—is literally "up there" coming "down here." "The Word became flesh and made his dwelling among us" (John 1:14).

The Good News is not that we're called to do these things on our own, as though we're being given a longer to-do list. The Good News is that a power has become available to increasingly turn us into the kind of people who naturally and recreationally do such things.

That's why when Jesus goes to Zacchaeus's house and Zacchaeus gives half his possessions to the poor and agrees to pay back all he has cheated four times over, Jesus says, "Today salvation has come to this house" (Luke 19:9). That doesn't just mean that Zacchaeus will be with God when he dies (although of course he will!). It means Jesus has come to this house, that up there is coming down here, because now—through Jesus—a corrupt tax collector has become a Kingdom bringer, the poor are being helped, the cheated are receiving justice, and God's will is being done on earth as it is in heaven.

The gospel—including the Good News of the Cross itself— means the renewal of all things. Miroslav Volf writes, "The cross is not forgiveness pure and simple, but God's setting aright the world of injustice and deception."[12] That is what the gospel announces. Starting with Zacchaeus. And you and me. — John Ortberg, *Eternity Is Now in Session: A Radical Rediscovery of What Jesus Really Taught about Salvation, Eternity, and Getting to the Good Place* (Carol Stream, IL: Tyndale Momentum, 2018).

17. His kingdom shall never end. What difference does it make? What are the implications?

The true Christian should often dwell on this glorious promise and take comfort in its contents. He has no cause to be ashamed of his Master. Poor and despised as he may often be for the Gospel's sake, he may feel assured that he is on the conquering side. The kingdoms of this world shall yet become the kingdoms of Christ. Yet a little time and He that shall come will come, and will not tarry. (Heb. 10:37.) For that blessed day let us patiently wait, and watch, and pray. Now is the time for carrying the cross, and for fellowship with Christ's sufferings. The day draws near when Christ shall take His great power and reign; and when all who have served Him faithfully shall exchange a cross for a crown. — J. C. Ryle, *Expository Thoughts on Luke, vol. 1* (New York: Robert Carter & Brothers, 1879), 25.

18. He will be great. From an historical perspective, how has this prophecy proven to be true?

Normally when someone dies, their impact on the world immediately begins to recede. As I write this, our world marks the passing of digital innovator Steve Jobs. Someone wrote that ten years ago our world had Bob Hope, Johnny Cash, and Steve Jobs; now we have no Jobs, no Cash, and no Hope. But Jesus inverted this normal human trajectory, as he did so many others. Jesus' impact was greater a hundred years after his death than during his life; it was greater still after five hundred years; after a thousand years his legacy laid the foundation for much of Europe; after two thousand years he has more followers in more places than ever.

If someone's legacy will outlast their life, it usually becomes apparent when they die. On the day when Alexander the Great or Caesar Augustus or Napoleon or Socrates or Mohammed died, their reputations were immense. When Jesus died, his tiny failed movement appeared clearly at an end. If there were a kind of "Most Likely to Posthumously Succeed" award given on the day of death to history's most influential people, Jesus would have come in dead last.

His life and teaching simply drew people to follow him. He made history by starting in a humble place, in a spirit of love and acceptance, and allowing each person space to respond. He deliberately placed himself on a collision course with Rome, where he would have been crushed like a gnat. And he was crushed.

And yet …

Jesus' vision of life continues to haunt and challenge humanity. His influence has swept over history like the tail of a comet, bringing his inspiration to influence art, science, government, medicine, and education; he has taught humans about dignity, compassion, forgiveness, and hope.

Since the day he did come — as G. K. Chesterton put it— "It has never been quite enough to say that God is in his heaven and all is right with the world; since the rumor is that God had left his heavens to set it right." — John Ortberg, *Who Is This Man? The Unpredictable Impact of the Inescapable Jesus* (Grand Rapids, MI: Zondervan, 2012).

19. How many movies have been made about Jesus's life? How many songs written?

He has been portrayed in movies by Frank Russell (1898), H. B. Warner, Jeffrey Hunter, Max von Sydow, Donald Sutherland, John Hurt, Willem Dafoe, Christian Bale, and Jim Caviezel as well as countless others. Songs about him have been sung by too many too count, from the first known song listed by the apostle Paul in the letter to the Philippians to an album ("Under the Mistletoe") released last Christmas by Justin Bieber.

— John Ortberg, *Who Is This Man? The Unpredictable Impact of the Inescapable Jesus* (Grand Rapids, MI: Zondervan, 2012).

20. Luke 1.32. Son of the Most High. What is that talking about?

He will be called the Son of the Most High.

John is described as the "prophet of the Most High" (Luke 1:76), whereas Jesus is declared as the "Son of the Most High." The fact that Jesus will be called "Son of the Most High" points to his equality with God. "Son of" is often used to refer to one who possesses his father's qualities. Jesus as the Son of the Most High possesses all the qualities of God the Father. — Ken Hemphill, *God Will* (Nashville, TN: B&H Academic, 2008).

21. What do you want to remember and apply from today's lesson?

22. How can we pray for each other this week?

Answers, Lesson #5
Aren't All Religions the Same?
Isaiah 44.6 – 17; John 14.5 - 7
Good Questions Have Groups Talking
www.joshhunt.com

Email your people to let them know we will be discussing the question: Are all religions basically alike. Ask them to do some googling and reading about the beliefs of major world religions. An informed group makes for interesting discussion.

OPEN

What friends have you known who were Buddhist, or Hindu or Muslim of some of other religion?

DIG

1. **Today, we will be looking at the topic: Are all religions alike? We are going to get into the biblical**

text in a moment, but, before we do, I'd like to look at the 4 largest world religions. They are:

- **Christianity: 2.1 billion.**

- **Islam: 1.3 billion.**

- **Hinduism: 900 million.**

- **Buddhism: 376 million.**

Let's start with Buddhism. What do you know about Buddhism? What do they believe? How does that differ from Christianity? http://www. primaryhomeworkhelp.co.uk/Religion.html

From its beginnings, Buddhism differed from most other religions. Rather than focusing on moral evil, it concentrated on pain and suffering; unlike other religions, Buddhism did not ask for devotion to or ritual toward a supreme god or gods. Buddhism is essentially a philosophy rather than a religion, an Eastern form of spirituality. David Bentley Taylor characterizes Buddhism as "a non-theistic ethical discipline, a system of self-training ... stressing ethics and mind-culture to the exclusion of theology."— James P. Eckman, *The Truth about Worldviews: A Biblical Understanding of Worldview Alternatives* (Wheaton, IL: Crossway Books, 2004), 37.

2. **Hinduism. Nearly a billion people call themselves Hindu. What do Hindus believe?**

Hinduism predates Buddhism by at least a thousand years and is one of the oldest world belief systems and the most baffling. It is unorganized, has no national church system, and embraces many contradictory beliefs, meaning different things to its vast number of devotees.

Hinduism traces its source to sacred scriptures called "the Vedas" (which means knowledge). This assortment of books is considered to be divinely inspired by Hindu gods and interpreted by ancient Hindu seers. This collection of religious literature bears the imprint of spiritistic influences.

Hinduism may be defined as the religious beliefs and practices common to India. One writer said that Hinduism is noted as being the only one of the major beliefs that cannot be defined.4 Another described it as a religion based on mythology because it has neither a founder (as do Buddhism, Islam, and Christianity) nor a fixed canon.5

But in spite of its diversity, Hinduism in general does reveal a number of common themes. Some of these include pantheism (the belief that all is God and God is all), polytheism (a belief in many lesser gods), and a reliance upon occultic ritual and practices.6

If you've ever pulled a thread from something you were wearing and had an entire seam unravel, you'll understand a little of the influence of Hinduism. If we grab some of its beliefs and give them a pull, a jumble of religious movements fall out. — David Jeremiah and Carole C. Carlson, *Invasion of Other Gods: The Seduction of New Age Spirituality* (Dallas: Word, 1995), 29.

3. **Next Islam. 1.3 billion and growing. What do they believe?**

   Monotheistic Islam shares many similarities with Judaism and Christianity, along with Zoroastrianism and Baha'i. But there are important differences. For example, Muslims share Judaism's belief in God's absolute oneness. Christians also believe God is one Being and that he eternally exists as three persons. The Qur'an and the Bible likewise agree on many of God's attributes, but again there are areas of disagreement. That the same or similar words are sometimes used with different meanings generates misunderstanding. For instance, Muslims and Christians both say God is merciful, but the Bible adds to this his grace and love. Minus these attributes, salvation as a divine gift is incomprehensible to Muslims.

All the monotheistic religions believe their scriptures to be a revelation from God. Muslims believe the revealing takes place by a process of dictation. The Qur'an, they say, exists eternally in heaven, and Gabriel came to earth and dictated the book to God's messenger Muhammad. Christians believe in a process called inspiration, from a Greek word meaning "God-breathed." The Holy Spirit inspired the Bible's human authors so that God's message is communicated while retaining the writers' individual styles and vocabulary.

These views have significant impact on thoughts about translation. The Bible was rendered into Syriac and Latin within a century of the New Testament's completion. Other translations followed; the combination of the printing press and the Protestant Reformation unleashed a tidal wave of translations into other languages. In contrast, the "true message" of the Qur'an can be read only in Arabic. Though translations exist, they're considered paraphrases, not authoritative. The many Muslims who don't read Arabic often use editions with parallel columns in Arabic and their own language.

Beliefs also vary as to the nature of humanity. While Christians believe everyone is born with a sin nature inherited from Adam and Eve, Muslims believe each person is born a clean slate and can choose to do either good or evil. The biblical creation account says humans were created in the image of God and given a mandate to be stewards of creation. For example, God brought all the animals to Adam, and whatever he called them became their name (Genesis 2:19–20). According to the Qur'an's account, God told Adam what the animal's names were, and Adam memorized them.

Regarding salvation, the Bible teaches that God has graciously provided salvation as a free gift to those who trust the righteousness of Jesus. No human effort can pay sin's penalty. Assurance of salvation is based on God's promises, because it is his work. The Qur'an teaches that whether someone goes to heaven or hell is ultimately up to God's will. By submitting to his will during this earthly life, one can hope to earn God's favor and will find out on Judgment Day whether or not it has been granted.

Perhaps most interesting, from a Christian viewpoint, are Muslim beliefs about Jesus. Islam acknowledges him as a great prophet, second only to Muhammad. But even Muslims are often unaware of all the Qur'an teaches about Jesus. First, it affirms his miraculous birth to the Virgin Mary. As is common in the Middle East to this day, the Qur'an refers to people by their first name and their father's name, using the Arabic word ibn. Jesus is the only person in the Qur'an identified by his mother's name. Second, he is given the title Masih, the Arabic equivalent of the English Messiah. The Arabic way of pronouncing his name is Isa, so in the Qur'an he is called "Isa Masih ibn Mariamu," Jesus the Messiah, the son of Mary.

Jesus is also described as a miracle-worker and is the only person the Qur'an mentions as living a sinless life. In the past century, as there has been more interaction between Christianity and Islam, Muslims are being taught that Muhammad also lived sinlessly. His confession of sin and uncertainty about the Day of Judgment in the Qur'an and Sunna, it is said, are examples for his followers. Further, it is now claimed that Muhammad also worked a miracle, being nonliterate yet producing the Qur'an, considered a masterpiece of Arabic literature.

The Qur'an teaches that Jesus ascended into heaven and is coming again at the resurrection day. With the Bible and the Qur'an both affirming so many aspects of his life, why are there two religions? Because the Qur'an also denies key biblical statements about Jesus. Muslims agree Jesus' conception was the work of God's Spirit in a virgin, but they disagree that this makes him anything other than an ordinary human. Islam denies his incarnation and deity and considers the term Son of God blasphemous.

Further, they understand the Qur'an to teach that Jesus did not die on a cross. God, they say, would never allow such a terrible thing to happen to one of his holy prophets. Without Jesus' death, there is, of course, no atonement for sin and no salvation. In fact, Islam denies even the possibility of one person being able to bear punishment for the sin of others. — Garry R. Morgan, *Understanding World Religions in 15 Minutes a Day* (Minneapolis, MN: Bethany House Publishers, 2012), 78–80.

4. **Let's talk about two more, because they are so strong in America: Mormonism and New Age. What do Mormons believe?**

Is Mormonism Christian? If the question asks only whether Mormonism is connected to Christianity in some sense, the answer would be "Yes." But that is not enough. Religions such as Baha'i claim some connection to Christianity, and Muslims believe in the second coming of Jesus. In order for a faith to be Christian it must pass both the doctrinal test and the experiential test. Doctrinally it must be orthodox on the key issues outlined above, and experientially it must see salvation as a faith encounter with Christ alone as the pathway to being right with God. How does Mormonism stack up?

Mormonism is neither monotheistic nor, technically, Trinitarian. In one of the Mormon scriptures, The Pearl of Great Price, we are told that the world was fashioned "by the gods." In his famous King Follett sermon, Joseph Smith stated that God was once as we are and that we may become as he is—a God. Mormonism teaches that Father, Son, and Spirit are all God, but it denies the historic Christian view on the Trinity. Mormon scholar Robert Millet has written that the Trinity is comprised of "Three Beings." Mormonism is not Trinitarian but tritheist. Mormon theology teaches that Jesus is an incarnation of Elohim, conceived as the literal son of God. But he is not the unique incarnation, since we also can be incarnations of the Father. Jesus is important to the whole of Mormon theology but in a different way than for traditional Christians. In Mormonism we are not saved by the atoning work of Christ but by obedience to Mormon principles. Mormons follow the Bible as Scripture, but they have placed three other texts alongside the Bible—The Book of Mormon, Doctrine and Covenants, and The Pearl of Great Price. It is in the last two books in particular that the novel Mormon doctrines can be found.

Because of these departures from standard Christian teachings, Mormonism falls outside orthodox Christianity. — Kenneth A. Mathews and A. Boyd Luter Jr., "Genesis," in *CSB Apologetics Study Bible*, ed. Ted Cabal (Nashville, TN: Holman Bible Publishers, 2017), 34.

5. New Age, by which I mean, roughly, the religion of Oprah. What is Oprah's theology?

In teaching psychology without theology, Oprah has become what someone called "a high priestess and icon of the psycholization of American society." When she features new age gurus on her show, she makes new age ideas seem mainstream to her millions of viewers worldwide. As one person says, "Oprah's clothes may bear labels, but her faith does not."[99]

According to new age thought, if I want to have a good self-image, I need affirmation; I need to feel good about myself, whether I should feel good about myself or not. I am the center of my world, I deserve to be happy, and I have the responsibility of making myself happy. I might be sleeping with my neighbor's spouse, but I should feel good about myself, managing my relationships as best I can.

But personal fulfillment cannot be found without a commitment to the hard principles of fidelity and God-honoring integrity. The worship of self excludes the worship of God. John Piper writes, "Our fatal error is believing that wanting to be happy means wanting to be made much of. It feels so good to be affirmed. But the good feeling is finally rooted in the worth of self, not the worth of God. This path to happiness is an illusion." — Erwin Lutzer, *Slandering Jesus: Six Lies People Tell about the Man Who Said He Was God* (Carol Stream, IL: Tyndale Momentum, 2016).

6. Let's talk about Christianity. Christians differ on lots of things. What is central to the Christian faith?

The Apostles' Creed is not found in the Bible. The Apostles' Creed was not written by the apostles. Rather, it was written at least 150 years after the apostles had all died. It is called the Apostles' Creed because it is supposed to be a record of what the apostles taught. The Apostles' Creed is as follows:

I believe in God, the Father Almighty,
the Creator of heaven and earth,
and in Jesus Christ, His only Son, our Lord:
Who was conceived of the Holy Spirit,
born of the Virgin Mary,
suffered under Pontius Pilate,
was crucified, died, and was buried.
He descended into hell.
The third day He arose again from the dead.
He ascended into heaven
and sits at the right hand of God the Father Almighty,
whence He shall come to judge the living and the dead.
I believe in the Holy Spirit, the holy catholic church,
the communion of saints,
the forgiveness of sins,
the resurrection of the body,
and life everlasting.
Amen.

The Apostles' Creed is a good summary of Christian doctrine. However, there are two primary concerns with the Apostles' Creed. First, in regards to the phrase "He descended into hell"—please see our article on "Did Jesus go to hell between His death and resurrection?" Second, in regards to "the holy catholic church," this does not refer to the Roman Catholic Church as we know it today. The word catholic means "universal." The true "catholic" church is all those who have placed their faith in Jesus Christ for salvation. Please see our article on the universal church. — Got Questions Ministries, *Got Questions? Bible Questions Answered* (Bellingham, WA: Logos Bible Software, 2002–2013).

7. Some say all religions are alike. Is that a reasonable statement?

Some people claim that all religions are essentially the same and only superficially different. The truth is, all religions are essentially different and only superficially the same.

Some say all religions are similar because they all teach ethics. The truth is that the other world religions fundamentally seek to help bad people become better by choosing better personal ethics. Christianity, on the other hand, invites spiritually dead people to become spiritually alive (John 3:5).

This is accomplished solely through Jesus' sacrificial death (2 Corinthians 5:21). Jesus claimed that what He said took precedence over all other people's teaching. He said He is humanity's only means of salvation (John 14:6). Those who followed Him confirmed this (Acts 4:12; 1 Timothy 2:5). Jesus also warned about those who would try to set forth a different Christ (Matthew 24:4-5).

The various religions also teach different views of God. Jesus taught about a triune God (Matthew 28:19). Muhammad (the founder of Islam) taught that the one God is not a Trinity. Hinduism refers to many gods that are extensions of the one impersonal Brahman. Buddhism teaches that the concept of God is essentially irrelevant. Obviously, these religions are not pointing to the same God. If one is right, the others are wrong. If Jesus was right (as Christians believe), the others are wrong. — Ron Rhodes, *5-Minute Apologetics for Today: 365 Quick Answers to Key Questions* (Eugene, OR: Harvest House Publishers, 2010).

8. Isaiah 44.6 – 17. What do we learn about the Christian Faith from this passage?

Jehovah or Yahweh (YHWH) is the special name given by God for himself in the Old Testament. It is the name revealed to Moses in Exodus 3:14, when God said, "I AM THAT I AM." While other titles for God may be used of men (Adonai [Lord] in Gen. 18:12) or false gods (elohim [gods] in Deut. 6:14), Jehovah is only used to refer to the one true God. No other person or thing was to be worshiped or served (Exod. 20:5), and his name and glory were not to be given to another. Isaiah wrote, "Thus saith Jehovah ... I am the first, and I am the last; and besides me there is no God" (Isa. 44:6 ASV)53 and, "I am Jehovah, that is my name; and my glory I will not give to another, neither my praise unto graven images" (42:8).

Yet Jesus claimed to be Jehovah on many occasions. Jesus prayed, "Father, glorify thou me in thy own presence with the glory which I had with thee before the world was made" (John 17:5). But Jehovah of the Old Testament says, "My glory I will not give to another" (Isa. 42:8). Jesus also declares, "I am the first and the last" (Rev. 1:17)—precisely the words Jehovah uses in Isaiah 42:8. Jesus says, "I am the good shepherd," (John 10:11), but the Old Testament says, "Jehovah is my shepherd" (Ps. 23:1). Further, Jesus claims to be the judge of all men (John 5:27f.; Matt. 25:31f.), but Joel quotes Jehovah as saying, "for there I will sit to judge all the nations round about" (Joel 3:12). Likewise, Jesus spoke of himself as the "bridegroom" (Matt. 25:1) while the Old Testament identifies Jehovah in this way (Isa. 62:5; Hos. 2:16). While the Psalmist declares, "Jehovah is our light" (Ps. 27:1), Jesus says, "I am the light of the world" (John 8:12).

Perhaps the strongest claim Jesus made to be Jehovah is in John 8:58, where he says, "Before Abraham was, I am." This statement claims not only existence before Abraham, but equality with the "I AM" of Exodus 3:14. The Jews around him clearly understood his meaning and picked up stones to kill him for blaspheming (cf. John 8:58; 10:31–33). The same claim is made in Mark 14:62 and John 18:5–6. — Norman L. Geisler and Abdul Saleeb, *Answering Islam: The Crescent in Light of the Cross, 2nd ed.* (Grand Rapids, MI: Baker Books, 2002), 249–250.

9. What do we learn about God?

The Hebrew for "I am the first and I am the last" is the same in Isaiah 44:6 and 48:12: וְרַחַא יֵבָא פַא וֹשאר יִנָא. This God is further identified as "the Yahweh of armies" in Isaiah 44:6.

The divine title "the first and the last" means that He is the first God and the last God because there are no other gods before or after Him. He alone is God.

The speaker in Isa. 48 is further identified by doing things which only God can do such as absolute foreknowledge (vs. 3, 5, 6), creation (v. 13), sovereignty (v. 15), and omnipresence (v. 16).

Who else but the one true God could say:

"For My own sake, for My own sake, I will act; For how can My name be profaned? And My glory I will not give to another." (Isa. 48:11) — Robert A. Morey, *The Trinity: Evidence and Issues* (Iowa Falls, IA: World Pub., 1996), 101.

10. Isaiah 44.8. One of the marks of God as Christians know Him is His ability to foretell the future. It is

impossible, for example, to read Isaiah 53 without thinking of Jesus on the cross. Look over Isaiah 53. Can you keep from seeing Jesus here? When was this written?

Throughout the Hebrew Scriptures, the promise of a Messiah is clearly given. These messianic prophecies were made hundreds, sometimes thousands of years before Jesus Christ was born, and clearly Jesus Christ is the only person who has ever walked this earth to fulfill them. In fact, from Genesis to Malachi, there are over 300 specific prophecies detailing the coming of this Anointed One. In addition to prophecies detailing His virgin birth, His birth in Bethlehem, His birth from the tribe of Judah, His lineage from King David, His sinless life, and His atoning work for the sins of His people, the death and resurrection of the Jewish Messiah was, likewise, well documented in the Hebrew prophetic Scriptures long before the death and resurrection of Jesus Christ occurred in history.

Of the best-known prophecies in the Hebrew Scriptures concerning the death of Messiah, Psalm 22 and Isaiah 53 certainly stand out. Psalm 22 is especially amazing since it predicted numerous separate elements about Jesus' crucifixion a thousand years before Jesus was crucified. Here are some examples. Messiah will have His hands and His feet "pierced" through (Psalm 22:16; John 20:25). The Messiah's bones will not be broken (a person's legs were usually broken after being crucified to speed up their death) (Psalm 22:17; John 19:33). Men will cast lots for Messiah's clothing (Psalm 22:18; Matthew 27:35).

Isaiah 53, the classic messianic prophecy known as the "Suffering Servant" prophecy, also details the death of Messiah for the sins of His people. More than 700 years before Jesus was even born, Isaiah provides details of His life and death. The Messiah will be rejected (Isaiah 53:3; Luke 13:34). The Messiah will be killed as a vicarious sacrifice for the sins of His people (Isaiah 53:5–9; 2 Corinthians 5:21). The Messiah will be silent in front of His accusers (Isaiah 53:7; 1 Peter 2:23). The Messiah will be buried with the rich (Isaiah 53:9; Matthew 27:57–60). The Messiah will be with criminals in His death (Isaiah 53:12; Mark 15:27). — Got Questions Ministries, *Got Questions? Bible Questions Answered* (Bellingham, WA: Logos Bible Software, 2002–2013).

11. **Another prophecy we looked at last week. An obscure, poor, uneducated virgin woman was told she would have a child and that child would be great. What are the odds? Let's review. What did we learn last week about the greatness of Jesus from an historical perspective?**

Normally when someone dies, their impact on the world immediately begins to recede. As I write this, our world marks the passing of digital innovator Steve Jobs. Someone wrote that ten years ago our world had Bob Hope, Johnny Cash, and Steve Jobs; now we have no Jobs, no Cash, and no Hope. But Jesus inverted this normal human trajectory, as he did so many others. Jesus' impact was greater a hundred years after his death than during his life; it was greater still after five hundred years; after a thousand years his legacy laid the foundation for much of Europe; after two thousand years he has more followers in more places than ever.

If someone's legacy will outlast their life, it usually becomes apparent when they die. On the day when Alexander the Great or Caesar Augustus or Napoleon or Socrates or Mohammed died, their reputations were immense. When Jesus died, his tiny failed movement appeared clearly at an end. If there were a kind of "Most Likely to Posthumously Succeed" award given on the day of death to history's most influential people, Jesus would have come in dead last.

His life and teaching simply drew people to follow him. He made history by starting in a humble place, in a spirit of love and acceptance, and allowing each person space to respond. He deliberately placed himself on a collision course with Rome, where he would have been crushed like a gnat. And he was crushed.

And yet ...

Jesus' vision of life continues to haunt and challenge humanity. His influence has swept over history like the tail of a comet, bringing his inspiration to influence art, science, government, medicine, and education; he has taught humans about dignity, compassion, forgiveness, and hope.

Since the day he did come — as G. K. Chesterton put it— "It has never been quite enough to say that God is in his heaven and all is right with the world; since the rumor is that God had left his heavens to set it right." — John Ortberg, *Who Is This Man? The Unpredictable Impact of the Inescapable Jesus* (Grand Rapids, MI: Zondervan, 2012).

12. He shall be great. We think He is great. How is life better for *everyone* because of Jesus?

Yale historian Jaroslav Pelikan wrote, "Regardless of what anyone may personally think or believe about him, Jesus of Nazareth has been the dominant figure in the history of Western Culture for almost twenty centuries. If it were possible, with some sort of super magnet, to pull up out of the history every scrap of metal bearing at least a trace of his name, how much would be left?

We live in a world where Jesus' impact is immense even if his name goes unmentioned. In some ways, our biggest challenge in gauging his influence is that we take for granted the ways in which our world has been shaped by him. G. K. Chesterton said that if you want to gauge the impact of his life, "The next best thing to being really inside Christendom is to be really outside it."

Children would be thought of differently because of Jesus. Historian O. M. Bakke wrote a study called When Children Became People: The Birth of Childhood in Early Christianity, in which he noted that in the ancient world, children usually didn't get named until the eighth day or so. Up until then there was a chance that the infant would be killed or left to die of exposure—particularly if it was deformed or of the unpreferred gender. This custom changed because of a group of people who remembered that they were followers of a man who said, "Let the little children come to me."

Jesus never married. But his treatment of women led to the formation of a community that was so congenial to women that they would join it in record numbers. In fact, the church was disparaged by its opponents for precisely that reason. Jesus' teachings about sexuality would lead to the dissolution of a sexual double standard that was actually encoded in Roman law.

Jesus never wrote a book. Yet his call to love God with all one's mind would lead to a community with such a reverence for learning that when the classical world was destroyed in what are sometimes called the Dark Ages, that little community would preserve what was left of its learning. In time, the movement he started would give rise to libraries and then guilds of learning.

Eventually Oxford and Cambridge and Harvard and Yale and virtually the entire Western system of education and scholarship would arise because of his followers. The insistence on universal literacy would grow out of an understanding that this Jesus, who was himself a teacher who highly praised truth, told his followers to enable every person in the world to learn.

He never held an office or led an army. He said that his kingdom was "not from this world." He was on the wrong side of the law at the beginning of his life and at its end. And yet the movement he started would eventually mean the end of emperor worship, be cited in documents like the Magna Carta, begin a tradition of common law and limited government, and undermine the power of the state rather than reinforce it as other religions in the empire had done. It is because of his movement that language such as "We hold these truths to be self-evident, that all men are created equal; that they are endowed by their Creator with certain unalienable rights" entered history.

The Roman Empire into which Jesus was born could be splendid but also cruel, especially for the malformed and diseased and enslaved. This one teacher had said, "Whatever you did for one of the least of these ..., you did for me." An idea slowly emerged that the suffering of every single individual human being matters and that those who are able to help ought to do so. Hospitals and relief efforts of all kinds emerged from this movement; even today they often carry names that remind us of him and his teachings.

Humility, which was scorned in the ancient world, became enshrined in a cross and was eventually championed as a virtue.

Enemies, who were thought to be worthy of vengeance ("help your friends and punish your enemies"), came to be seen as worthy of love. Forgiveness moved from weakness to an act of moral beauty.

Even in death, Jesus' influence is hard to escape. The practice of burial in graveyards or cemeteries was taken from his followers; cemetery itself comes from a Greek word meaning "sleeping place." It expressed the hope of resurrection. If there is a tombstone, it will often have the date of birth and the date of death with a dash in between, the length of that human life measured by its distance from Jesus' lifetime. In many cases, if a tombstone is unaffordable, a grave is marked with a cross, a reminder of Jesus' death. To this day, if a cartoonist wants a shorthand way of referring to the afterlife, a simple sketch of Saint Peter in the clouds by a pearly gate will be understood. Whatever it did or did not do to his existence, death did not end Jesus' influence. In many ways, it just started it. — John Ortberg, *Who Is This Man? The Unpredictable Impact of the Inescapable Jesus* (Grand Rapids, MI: Zondervan, 2012).

13. John 14.5 – 7. What do we learn about Jesus from this passage?

However far we may drift, we must always come back to these words of our Lord: "I am the way"—not a road that we leave behind us, but the way itself. Jesus Christ is the way of God, not a way that leads to God; that is why He says—"Come unto Me," "abide in Me." "I am . . . the truth," not the truth about God, not a set of principles, but the truth itself. Jesus Christ is the Truth of God. "No man cometh unto the Father, but by Me." We can get to God as Creator in other ways, but no man can come to God as Father in any other way than by

Jesus Christ (cf. Matthew 11:27). "I am . . . the life." Jesus Christ is the Life of God as He is the Way and the Truth of God. Eternal life is not a gift from God, it is the gift of God Himself. The life imparted to me by Jesus is the life of God. "He that hath the Son hath the life"; "I am come that they might have life"; "And this is life eternal, that they should know Thee the only true God" (rv). We have to abide in the way; to be incorporated into the truth ; to be infused by the life. — Oswald Chambers, *So Send I You: The Secret of the Burning Heart* (Hants UK: Marshall, Morgan & Scott, 1930).

14. I am the way, the truth, and the life. Let's look at each of these separately. Jesus is the way. The way to what?

The problem is that many of us have majored on only one-third of this amazing, self-disclosing, God-revealing decree. It seems we have developed a fetish for the truth. Churches offer what they think is the right doctrine instead of helping people discover the life Jesus came to give. We fight over dogma, insisting that believing the right thing will yield the right life. The truth is, the Pharisees in Jesus' day did the same thing so many Christians are doing today. We are on information overload. We go to Bible studies, attend seminars, and listen to countless sermons, but this one reality remains: Information and the amassing of information, no matter how true it is, does not lead to life transformation.

We have believed that the pursuit of truth alone will yield a life worth living, and so we have emphasized doctrine over life, facts over vitality, and information over transformation. Because of our relentless pursuit to get everything right, we've gotten it all wrong.

Transformation is an experience. It's something that happens to a person who alters the trajectory and quality of life from that point forward. It's transformation that we most need to live the life we most want. Paul, the writer of most of the New Testament, was transformed by the experience of meeting Jesus on the dusty road to Damascus. His head was already filled with all sorts of erroneous knowledge. What he lacked was the experience of meeting Jesus. Everything changed for Paul after that encounter. It's my hope that this book will be a Damascus Road encounter for you. I want you to meet Jesus in a whole new way—not just the Jesus who died but the Jesus who really lived! As I've pondered and practiced these ways, the life I most need and the life that is most sacred is returning to my heart. I want this for you, too. As we intentionally practice these ways, we find ourselves not only recovering but also experiencing and living the life Jesus offers us. Remember, Jesus did not come to just teach us new truths so that we can believe; He came to show us how to live. — Stephen W. Smith, *The Jesus Life: Eight Ways to Recover Authentic Christianity* (Colorado Springs, CO: David C Cook, 2012).

15. The truth. What did Jesus mean by saying he was the truth?

In addition to being the Way and the Life, in this statement Jesus reveals Himself as the Truth. He tells His disciples that He is the source, the normative standard of truth. Without Him, mankind would know nothing at all, and in coming to Him, His disciples arrive at the Truth itself. Because Jesus is the Truth itself, we can be confident regarding everything He says. We can be confident not only in His teachings recorded in the gospels but also the teachings found in the rest of the Bible. This is because Jesus tells us that all the Scriptures are inspired by God (Matt. 4:4;19:3–6). We can stand on Scripture's teaching because the Truth Himself confirms it. — Tabletalk Magazine, *January 2004: The Letter to the Hebrews* (Lake Mary, FL: Ligonier Ministries, 2004), 39.

16. John 8.31 - 32. Another review question. How do we hold to Jesus teachings (John 8.31 NIV)? What benefits come to those who do?

No Spiritual Discipline is more important than the intake of God's Word. Nothing can substitute for it. There simply is no healthy Christian life apart from a diet of the milk and meat of Scripture. The reasons for this are obvious. In the Bible God tells us about Himself, and especially about Jesus Christ, the incarnation of God. The Bible unfolds the Law of God to us and shows us how we've all broken it. There we learn how Christ died as a sinless, willing Substitute for breakers of God's Law and how we must repent and believe in Him to be right with God. In the Bible we learn the ways and will of the Lord. We find in Scripture how to live in a way that is pleasing to God as well as best and most fulfilling for ourselves. None of this eternally essential information can be found anywhere else except the Bible. Therefore if we would know God and be Godly, we must know the Word of God—intimately. — Donald S. Whitney, *Spiritual Disciplines for the Christian Life* (Colorado Springs, CO: NavPress, 1991), 28.

17. Jesus said He is the life. What does that mean?

This world can be a better place. God wants everyday people like you and me to make this world just a bit more like heaven.

In one small corner of His grand creation, God created a place that was a lot like heaven. He named it Eden. The Garden State was not just beautiful, it was perfect—a piece of heaven on earth. Pain was absent, poverty was unheard of, food was everywhere, and disease was nowhere … and best of all, everybody (well, all two of them) walked close to God.

However, being the humans we are, things went sideways. We tried to deceive God. This one act, this one moment changed everything. This wrongness called sin began to spread and multiply and reproduce like a mutating virus.1

But here's the good news in all of this—life can still be beautiful. God is still present, and He's doing good today through people who love Him and want to love others in the same way His Son loved you and me.

We all have this feeling deep in our souls that life can be different, that life can be so much more beautiful than it is. Families are not supposed to be broken. Children are not supposed to be abandoned when their mothers die from AIDS. Fathers are not supposed to lose their jobs. Women are not supposed to be held back because of their gender. And people should never experience prejudice because of their race.

God has a more beautiful way.

John Ortberg, in his deeply insightful way, explains the rich meaning behind the ancient Hebrew word shalom.2 The Old Testament prophets spoke about a coming day when God would change the way things are and make this world beautiful again; to describe this, the Jews used the word shalom.3 The word literally means "to be perfect or complete." When the Jews dream about peace they use the word shalom. When King David wrote about peace, he used the word shalom. The word can mean safe. Or maybe this says it best—when life is just right. — Palmer Chinchen, *True Religion: Taking Pieces of Heaven to Places of Hell on Earth* (Colorado Springs, CO: David C. Cook, 2010).

18. Some say that Jesus is one way. You say?

I am trying here to prevent anyone saying the really foolish thing that people often say about Him: 'I'm ready to accept Jesus as a great moral teacher, but I don't accept His claim to be God.' That is the one thing we must not say. A man who was merely a man and said the sort of things Jesus said would not be a great moral teacher. He would either be a lunatic—on a level with the man who says he is a poached egg—or else he would be the Devil of Hell. You must make your choice. Either this man was, and is, the Son of God: or else a madman or something worse. You can shut Him up for a fool, you can spit at Him and kill Him as a demon; or you can fall at His feet and call Him Lord and God. But let us not come with any patronising nonsense about His being a great human teacher. He has not left that open to us. He did not intend to. — C. S. Lewis, *Mere Christianity* (New York: HarperOne, 2001), 52.

19. What did you learn today? What do you want to remember?

20. How can we pray for each other this week?

Answers, Lesson #6
The Power of Your Story / Acts 26
Good Questions Have Groups Talking
www.joshhunt.com

OPEN

Who do you know that you are pray for as far as them coming to know Christ?

DIG

1. **One of the most powerful tools for evangelism is the power of your story. Today, we want to learn about how to tell our story from looking at the way Paul told his story. Before we get into that, why is story such a powerful thing?**

    You may not realize the power of your story or the influence you can have with it, but you have a story to share, and there is no one who can tell it better than you! Chances are, you are a lot more inspiring than you give yourself credit for. There are people out there who need to hear your story for hope, healing, encouragement, and direction to God. — Doug Fields, *Fresh Start: God's Invitation to a Great Life* (Nashville: Thomas Nelson, 2011).

2. **In church world, we generally call this story a testimony. How is sharing your testimony different from sharing the gospel?**

When we speak of sharing your story or telling your testimony, we are talking about proclaiming to others how you came to Christ. You are giving a witness. "In a courtroom, a witness isn't expected to argue a case, prove the truth or press for a verdict; that is the job of the attorneys. Witnesses simply report what happened to them or what they saw."1

Every believer has a testimony. If you have been saved, you have a salvation story. Granted, some may be more dramatic than others, yet there are people who need to hear your story. No one else's story is exactly like yours, so you need to share it, or it will be lost forever. — Dave Earley and David Wheeler, *Evangelism Is* . . . (Nashville, TN: B&H Academic, 2010).

3. **As we read this passage, I'd like to ask you to look for three things: before, how, and after. What was Paul's life like before Christ? How did he come to Christ? What was his life after coming to Christ?**

In our evangelism training courses, David Wheeler and I have our students write their testimony out using three main points.

1.   What my life was like before Christ

2.   How I met Christ as Savior

3.   How Christ changed my life

I have students practice sharing their stories in a minute—three 20-second sections. We also have them write their testimonies in a paper. They can do it in less than a thousand words. Many love this project because in writing their testimony they realize what God has done for them. They realize that they do have a story and, after writing it down, feel much more confident in sharing it. — Dave Earley and David Wheeler, *Evangelism Is . . .* (Nashville, TN: B&H Academic, 2010).

4. **Agrippa. What do we know about Agrippa? You might see if your Study Bible has a note.**

King Agrippa II was the latest of the Herod Dynasty, the last of the Herods to meddle with Christ or his followers. His great-grandfather was the King Herod who had feared the birth of the Christ-child and murdered the male children in the vicinity of Bethlehem. The grand-uncle of Agrippa II had murdered John the Baptist, and his father, Agrippa I, had executed James and imprisoned Peter and was eaten with worms as punishment for allowing people to worship him as a god right there in Caesarea (12:20–23).[1]

With Agrippa was Bernice, his sister, who was one year younger. She had once been engaged to Marcus, a nephew of the philosopher Philo. Then she married her uncle—Herod, King of Chalcis. But now she was living incestuously with her full blood brother Agrippa. So notorious was her conduct that when she later became the Emperor Titus' mistress, he had to send her away because of the moral outcry of pagan Rome.[2] Agrippa and Bernice were a sick, sin-infested couple.

To make matters even more outrageous, Rome considered Agrippa an authority on the Jewish religion. Because he was a Herod, he was appointed curator of the temple and thus had the power to appoint the high priest and to administer the temple treasury. — R. Kent Hughes, *Acts: The Church Afire, Preaching the Word* (Wheaton, IL: Crossway Books, 1996), 326.

5. Acts 26.2. What do you sense is Paul's tone as he tells his story?

What a gracious, disarming opening statement! No narrow-minded fire-and-brimstone words of condemnation flew from Paul's lips. That wasn't his style. Courteously, he said he considered the entire ordeal a wonderful privilege.

Right out of the chute, we can learn a lesson from our hero Paul. When God grants us the rare opportunity to stand before prestigious people and high-ranking government officials, it is best to demonstrate courtesy and grace. Regardless of their lifestyle, speak with respect. Regardless of their politics or their private world, model grace. Show some class.

To come on like gangbusters will surely be an offense, and the door of opportunity will slam shut. Paul didn't roar at his audience, even though they lived lives altogether different than he would approve. Despite his chains and their differences, he addressed them with kindness and respect. — Charles R. Swindoll, *Paul: A Man of Grace and Grit* (Nashville: Thomas Nelson, 2009).

6. How important is tone as we tell our story?

The tone of your voice has more to do with your success in dealing with conflict than any other factor. If you respond to another person in a sarcastic or snippy manner, he or she will perceive that tone in your voice and retaliate. Even if you are right, you and the other person will end up losing because feelings will be hurt, and you will cause damage to your relationship. You are never justified in using a snippy tone, no matter how much you try to rationalize to yourself that you are.

Research shows that parents who use a harsh tone with their teenagers have more problems with them. Their children are also more likely to experience depression than those from their softer-spoken counterparts. Shouting at your child will not improve his or her behavior.29 What will make a difference are consequences. Not nagging or a harsh tone, but specific penalties you enforce for improper behavior.

Memorize Proverbs 15:1. Post it on your mirror. Make it your screen saver on your computer. Meditate on it as you go to sleep at night. It is without doubt the most powerful principle to consider when dealing with conflict, and you can apply it before, during, and after a disagreement arises. — Steve Reynolds, *Wise Up*, 2014.

7. What was Paul's life like before Christ?

Paul begins by talking about his life in Judaism, and what he stresses here is that he was a faithful Jew. He had been raised a Jew, having received the traditions of the Jews from his fathers. He knew the law. So far as he knew and understood the law, he had lived by it.

He had lived according to the strictest sect of his day. He was a Pharisee. We have a bad view of the Pharisees because Jesus called them "hypocrites, ... whitewashed tombs, which look beautiful on the outside but on the inside are full of dead men's bones." That was right. Many of them were exactly that. As a matter of fact, it is a proper description of the entire human race. We are all hypocrites. Yet in their day the Pharisees had a good reputation because they were what we would call "fundamentalists." They were the conservatives of their day. They said, "We believe in the inerrancy of the Bible. We believe everything that is written there." They really did, at least so far as they understood it.

Paul's defense was that the only things he was proclaiming were what was in the law, things well understood by the Jews—at least those who believed the Old Testament Scriptures, as the Pharisees did.

Paul's chief point was the promise of the resurrection. He interrupted his address at this point to ask wisely, "Why should any of you consider it incredible that God raises the dead?" (26:8). We are going to see, as the story continues, that his Gentile hearers did consider the resurrection to be incredible, just as people consider it incredible today. But Paul was a Jew, raised on the Scriptures, and the Jews as a whole (and the Pharisees in particular) believed in the supernatural. — James Montgomery Boice, *Acts: An Expositional Commentary* (Grand Rapids, MI: Baker Books, 1997), 404–405.

8. Verse 12ff. How did Paul's life change?

The second part of Paul's address concerns his conversion and the commission God gave him. There have been a number of attempts by unbelievers to explain what happened to the apostle Paul on the road to Damascus, eliminating the fact that the Second Person of the Trinity, incarnate and now risen from the dead, actually appeared to him. Some have said, quite seriously, that Paul probably had epilepsy. His experience on the road to Damascus was actually an epileptic fit.

Some have imagined that he had heatstroke. The sun was bright. It was hot. No doubt, these conditions overcame him.

When I think of these far-out, desperate arguments, I remember what Harry Ironside said when he dealt with them in his collection of sermons on the Book of Acts. He quoted Spurgeon as saying, "Oh, blessed epilepsy that made such a wonderful change in this man! Would

God that all who oppose the name of Jesus Christ might become epileptics in the same sense." After referring to the sunstroke idea, Ironside wrote: "Would God that all modernists could be so sunstruck that they might begin to preach Christ, and so come back to the grand old gospel of redemption by the blood of Jesus!" Then, in what I suppose was a bit of whimsy, Ironside said, "And yet ... I am quite in agreement with the modernists save for one letter. It was a Son-stroke, not a sun-stroke! It was the light of the glory of God in the face of Christ Jesus that struck home to the very heart of that man and gave him to see the One he had been persecuting—the Savior of sinners."1

The apostle Paul was turned around. He could testify to the grace of God in his transformation. If the Lord Jesus Christ has stopped you and turned you around, then you can testify too. If you are not testifying to God's grace or if you feel you cannot, you need to examine yourself to see whether you have really met Jesus. Has Jesus turned you from sin? Has he revealed himself to you? Have you come to trust him? — James Montgomery Boice, *Acts: An Expositional Commentary* (Grand Rapids, MI: Baker Books, 1997), 405.

9. **Acts 26.19. After. What do we learn about conversion from Paul's "After" part of his story?**

The third part of Paul's defense before King Agrippa had to do with his service for Christ following his conversion.

The first thing he stresses is his obedience, though he couches it in negative form: "So then, King Agrippa, I was not disobedient to the vision from heaven" (26:19). One of the first marks of our conversion is that we obey Jesus Christ. We might even call it the first mark, except that faith itself is the first evidence. Are you obeying Jesus? Jesus said, "Why do you call me, 'Lord, Lord,' and do not do what I say?" (Luke 6:46). If you are disobeying Jesus, you are not his disciple. If you are not his disciple, you are not saved. People who have heard the voice of Jesus Christ just do not ignore it. — James Montgomery Boice, *Acts: An Expositional Commentary* (Grand Rapids, MI: Baker Books, 1997), 405.

10. Acts 26.20. How does this verse compare with Acts 1.8? What is the lesson for us?

Second, Paul talks about the scope of his ministry, indicating that it widened more and more as God worked through him to reach others (26:20). I find it interesting that here in the twenty-sixth chapter of this book, after we have been through all the history that Luke has recorded concerning the expansion of the gospel, we find the apostle Paul describing the sphere of his ministry in almost the same terms as the Lord Jesus Christ used when he gave his missionary charge to the disciples before Pentecost (Acts 1:8). Paul had been doing what Jesus described. Why? Because he was obedient to the Lord, and that is what Jesus had said his people were to do. — James Montgomery Boice, *Acts: An Expositional Commentary* (Grand Rapids, MI: Baker Books, 1997), 406.

11. Acts 26.22ff. What do we learn about sharing our story from this part of Paul's story?

The third thing Paul says when he talks about his service following his conversion is that he preached the gospel. He proclaimed "nothing beyond what the prophets and Moses said would happen" (26:22). What was that?

First, that "Christ would suffer"—that is, die. This was a testimony to the atonement.

Second, that Jesus would "rise from the dead."

Third, that being raised from the dead, he "would proclaim light to his own people and to the Gentiles" (26:23). This happened through witnesses like Paul.

What should our response to such a gospel be? Paul gives this as well, no doubt for the explicit benefit of King Agrippa, Festus, and the others. He says that the Gentiles should "repent," "turn to God," and "prove their repentance by their deeds" (26:20). — James Montgomery Boice, *Acts: An Expositional Commentary* (Grand Rapids, MI: Baker Books, 1997), 406.

12. Back up to Acts 26.20. Repent. This is key. What does it mean to repent? Does it mean to be sad? Does it mean to cry? Is it emotional? What does repent mean?

What should our response to such a gospel be? Paul gives this as well, no doubt for the explicit benefit of King Agrippa, Festus, and the others. He says that the Gentiles should "repent," "turn to God," and "prove their repentance by their deeds" (26:20).

To repent means "to turn around." If you are going in one direction and repent, you turn around and go another direction. It is the equivalent of conversion, which means the same thing. It is what had happened to Paul on the road to Damascus. He was going one way, but God turned him around so that he went in a different way entirely. That needs to happen to everyone who would find salvation in Christ. — James Montgomery Boice, *Acts: An Expositional Commentary* (Grand Rapids, MI: Baker Books, 1997), 406.

13. Some say repentance sounds so negative. You say?

Turning from sin and going in another way also means "turning to God." Christianity is not just negative. It is not just "sin not" or "abandon your current lifestyle." Christianity is positive. It means finding righteousness and a new life in Christ. This new life is not only different but better. It is a life lived in and with God. — James Montgomery Boice, *Acts: An Expositional Commentary* (Grand Rapids, MI: Baker Books, 1997), 406.

14. Repentance is so important. How do we know if we got it right? How do w know if we have truly repented?

Then, lest there be anything like cheap grace, easy repentance, or a mere verbal profession, Paul also said that Gentiles need to "prove their repentance by their deeds." How do you know if you are a Christian or not? Do you know it simply because you can mouth the right words? Hardly. We can fool ourselves into mouthing just about anything. We know we are Christians when our lives are changed and we begin to do good works. That is the proof—when we begin to follow after Jesus Christ and obey him. — James Montgomery Boice, *Acts: An Expositional Commentary* (Grand Rapids, MI: Baker Books, 1997), 406.

15. How did Festus respond to Paul's story?

In the late 1800s a clergyman by the name of Bishop Wright thought it was impossible for man to fly. "Flight," he said, "is reserved for the angels." On December 17, 1903 his oldest son, Wilbur, took his seat in the first power-driven plane ever built and was airborne at Kitty Hawk, North Carolina, for twelve seconds and 120 feet. There were some who thought the Wright brothers were a little touched before that fateful day, but today they are everyone's heroes.

It was the same for Christopher Columbus. People were so sure this crazy explorer would sail off the end of the earth that many of their coins carried the Latin inscription, "Ne Plus Ultra"—"no more beyond." After 1492 when he sailed the ocean blue, the new coins read "Plus Ultra"—"more beyond."

When Robert Fulton gave his first public demonstration of his steamboat, some bystanders chanted, "It will never start, never start, never start…" When it started, the astonished crowd began to repeat, "It will never stop, never stop, never stop…"

Similarly, many of the Apostle Paul's contemporaries considered him out of touch with reality. Even today some maintain that Paul had a hallucination on the Damascus Road and that his subsequent teachings perverted Judaism. But the fact of the matter is, Paul was the sanest of theologians, and his teachings were anointed by God.

Acts 26 records Paul's sanity being questioned. Besides the great apostle, the cast of characters in this divinely orchestrated drama includes Festus, whom we met in Acts 25, and Agrippa and Bernice, a couple who were even more unsavory than Felix and Drusilla. — R. Kent Hughes, *Acts: The Church Afire, Preaching the Word* (Wheaton, IL: Crossway Books, 1996), 325.

16. **Let's prepare ourselves to share our story by learning from how Paul told his story. First, before. What was your life like before Christ?**

Here are practical suggestions for developing the before, how, and after sections in your personal testimony.

1. Before:

a. Many people's actions spring out of their unsatisfied deep inner needs. What were one or two of your unsatisfied deep inner needs before you came to know Jesus Christ? Some examples of inner needs are:

_ lack of peace
_ fear of death
_ something missing
_ no meaning to life
_ desire to be in control
_ loneliness
_ lack of security
_ lack of purpose
_ lack of significance
_ no real friends
_ no motivation

Discipleship Journal, Issue 60 (November/December 1990) (NavPress, 1990).

17. What if you came to faith early in life and don't have a lot of "before" material? What would your testimony look like then?

Format Three: Early Conversion, Consistent Growth

Before

As I look around me I see people feverishly trying to fill voids in their lives. Men are giving themselves to their jobs, and in the process sacrificing their families. A number of my fellow workers seem to be trying to find meaning in their lives, but just when they think they have attained what they want, they realize these things are not meeting their deepest needs. I find myself being involved in many of these same activities, but I am finding satisfaction. What is the difference?

How

I realize that I'm not reacting to life the way many people do for a good reason. I have something in my life that has given me peace and purpose that many others do not have. I have discovered that a personal relationship with Jesus Christ fills the voids that many people are trying to fill with activities and things that just don't satisfy.

As I was growing up, my parents were very active in church. Because they were active, they figured that I should be also. So every Sunday, there we were. What was real to them was just a game to me. Then one summer I attended a church summer camp. This changed my whole view of "religion." I discovered at this camp that Christianity was more than a religion, it was a personal relationship with God through His Son, Jesus Christ. In the evenings our discussions centered around who Jesus Christ was and what He did. They were interesting to me. One day after we had finished sports my counselor asked me if I had ever personally committed my life to Jesus Christ or if I was still thinking about it. I told him I was still thinking about it. We sat down and talked. He explained from the Bible what I would need to do to become a real Christian. I saw that I had done many things wrong and that the penalty was eternal death! I saw that Christ had died on the cross to set me free from that penalty. I prayed with my counselor right there and committed my life to Jesus Christ.

After

As I grew physically I also grew spiritually. I find that when I try to do things my way and leave God out of the picture, I have the same struggles as everyone else. But when I let Him be in control, I experience a peace that can only come from Him. But the greatest thing of all is that I know for certain that I have eternal life. — *Discipleship Journal, Issue 60* (November/December 1990) (NavPress, 1990).

18. How did you come to faith in Christ?

How:

a. Describe the circumstances that caused you to consider Christ as the solution to your deep inner needs. Identify the events that led to your conversion. In some cases this may have taken place over a period of time.

b. State specifically the steps you took to become a Christian. If there is a particular passage of Scripture that applies here, you may want to use it. Usually you will simply paraphrase it.

c. Include the gospel clearly and briefly. The gospel includes:

- All have sinned

- Sin's penalty

- Christ paid the penalty

- Must receive Christ

Discipleship Journal, Issue 60 (November/December 1990) (NavPress, 1990).

19. How has life been following Christ? What do you love about following Christ?

1. State how Christ filled or is filling your deep inner needs. In the before, you expressed your needs and how you tried unsuccessfully to meet them. You now

want to briefly show the difference that Christ has made in your life.

2. Conclude with a statement like: "But the greatest benefit is that I know for certain that I have eternal life." The person you talk to will tend to comment on the last thing you say. Often it is natural to move from the testimony into a clear presentation of the gospel. — *Discipleship Journal, Issue 60* (November/December 1990) (NavPress, 1990).

20. How can we pray for each other this week?